PRESENTED TO:

_____

FROM:

_____

DATE:

_____

WISDOM

fROM A

pASTOR'S

HEART

Douglas connelly

JOSSEY-BASS
A Wiley Company
San Francisco

JOSSEY-BASS
A Wiley Company
San Francisco

Jossey-Bass books and products are available through most bookstores. To contact Jossey-Bass directly, call (888) 378-2537, fax to (800) 605-2665, or visit our website at www.josseybass.com.

Substantial discounts on bulk quantities of Jossey-Bass books are available to corporations, professional associations, and other organizations. For details and discount information, contact the special sales department at Jossey-Bass.

Unless otherwise noted, the scripture quotations contained herein are from the New Revised Standard Version of the Bible, copyright 1989, by the Division of Christian Education of the National Council of Churches of Christ in the U.S.A. Used by permission. All rights reserved.

We have made all reasonable efforts to locate the copyright owners of sermons reprinted in this book from previous volumes of *The Minister's Manual.* We are prepared to fully credit the source in future reprints and pay appropriate fees for inclusion in this volume. Please contact the publisher.

We at Jossey-Bass strive to use the most environmentally sensitive paper stocks available to us. Our publications are printed on acid-free recycled stock whenever possible, and our paper always meets or exceeds minimum GPO and EPA requirements.

Library of Congress Cataloging-in-Publication Data

Conelly, Douglas, date
    Wisdom from a pastor's heart / Douglas Connelly.—1st ed.
       p.   cm.
    ISBN 0-7879-5651-1 (alk. paper)
    1. Christian life. I. Title
    BV4501.3 .C66 2001
    242—dc21   2001-02429

FIRST EDITION
HB Printing   10 9 8 7 6 5 4 3 2 1

contents

IN THE SHADOW AND IN THE LIGHT

PREFACE

or more than seventy-five years, *The Minister's Manual* (under the capable guidance of a series of editors) has provided insight and inspiration to pastors and church leaders as they have ministered to their congregations. But the collected wisdom of these hundreds of Christian teachers has been largely forgotten as each new annual volume has been produced. I have had the privilege of selecting from these rich reserves passages that speak directly and poignantly to the hearts and souls of contemporary Christians. My intention has been to create an inspirational book that will give readers the comfort of a kind and wise pastoral companion, one who can address the many facets of being a Christian through insight, reflection, and prayer.

I have grouped the selections from *The Minister's Manual* into three sections and under thirty topics that touch our lives—topics such as marriage, parenting, forgiveness, and anger. You will be blessed, comforted, encouraged, and challenged as you read and meditate on the wisdom in these pages. One guiding principle directed me as I selected passages to be included in the book. I kept asking myself, *In what areas of life do we Christians need the guidance of a wise pastor, and what would that pastor say to us?* Reading this book is like having a "pastor in your pocket," as gifted spiritual leaders share their encouragement and advice.

Please keep in mind that there is no right way to read this book. You may want to start at the beginning and read a section each day, or you may want to find a section that speaks to a particular area of life with which you are struggling right now. Whichever approach you choose, I think you will come back to these pages again and again as you walk the pathway of faith. Enjoy the journey!

❖ A NOTE ON SOURCES ❖

I am indeed fortunate to have, and am grateful for, the seventy-five editions of *The Minister's Manual* to draw on in creating *Wisdom from a Pastor's Heart.* As I carefully selected materials from the volumes in this series, I was struck once again not only by the wisdom in these pages but also by the fact that few Christians have had access to these accumulated riches. Some of the materials were created decades ago yet retain their freshness and value for today. This new volume allows these gifted Christian teachers and ministers to speak to us once again.

The name of the author or original source is noted directly following most of the selections in this book. In older volumes of *The Minister's Manual,* some sermons and prayers had no author's name attached to them. I have credited the creators of all these materials to the extent that I am able. Both Jossey-Bass and I have made every effort possible to locate these writers before including their work in this volume, but because of the amount of time that has passed and the lack of records, we have not always been able to do so. If anyone identifies material that has been used here without their express permission, please make it known to me and we will gladly send a free copy of Carol M. Norén's *In Times of Crisis and Sorrow—A Minister's Manual Resource Guide* and make whatever other amends are appropriate.

❧ A WORD OF THANKS ❧

The opportunity to compile the material for this book came at a tough transition time in my life. Reading the spiritual wisdom in the seventy-five volumes of *The Minister's Manual* brought refreshment and insight when I needed them most. My wife, Karen, and I were encouraged and blessed each day as we read through that day's selections. Faithful friends blessed our lives, too, and I dedicate this book to them: Ken and Carole, Bill and Linda, Don and Susan, Don and Shelby, Jerry and Jenny. I also want to thank Sheryl Fullerton, my editor at Jossey-Bass, for her confidence in my abilities and for her encouragement at every stage of the book's development.

Flushing, Michigan   Douglas Connelly
July 2001

WISDOM

FROM A PASTOR'S

HEART

❧ ❧

the
journey
of faith

❧ ❧

Most of us long for companionship with God. We have all had moments when God has touched our lives, when we have sensed his power in a thunderstorm or his protection in an accident or his love when our world has seemed to be caving in. As wonderful as those moments have been, however, they have only made us hunger for more, for a deeper intimacy with God. We want assurance that we are not taking the journey through life alone.

The chapters in this section focus on the journey, the walk of faith. Some of the selections are meant to awaken us and prepare us for new challenges that lie just ahead. Other selections warn us of danger or lead us to a place of rest. In some passages, we may find insight into what is required of us at the particular place in which we find ourselves at this moment. A few of these wise words will bring a startling flood of grace—refreshment to our thirsty souls.

"O LORD, MY ROCK"

faith

❧ ❧

Steadfast love surrounds those who trust in the Lord.

PSALM 32:10

Trust in the Lord forever,
for in the Lord God
you have an everlasting rock.

ISAIAH 26:4

Trust in God, faith, is the firm foundation under everything that makes life worth living.

HEBREWS 11:1, *THE MESSAGE*

❧ ❧

The first Christians called themselves believers *(Acts 2:44)—they had come to believe in Jesus as Savior and Lord. The Christian life begins with an act of faith, but it doesn't end there. We also walk through life by faith. We have confidence in God's character—in his grace and his goodness. We accept the truth of God's Word to us in the Bible. We rest in God's promise to forgive us through the sacrifice of Jesus on the cross. We rely on God to guide us and help us through difficult times. All of these are acts of faith. Faith is not closing our eyes to reality; it is opening our eyes to God's reality.*

❧ ❧

Faith as the Bible describes it looks a lot like courage. Faith is the courage to go out and meet the giants in your life. Faith trusts in God alone.

Mark Trotter

❖ ❖

The smallest level of faith, Jesus said to a group of frustrated disciples, is enough to move mountains. Mountains! What kind of mountains? Jesus is not talking about moving Mount Mc-Kinley. He is saying that faith the size of a seed can move the mountains blocking the horizons of our hopes, shadowing the light and beauty of love, limiting and bounding the scope of our lives. He is saying that faith can stand up and move—or remove—the things that trap us, the stuff that scares the daylights out of us, the things that test and erode our confidence in God's love for us.

James W. Crawford

❖ ❖

Faith means hanging on when there seems to be nothing on which to hang. When we have done all we can do, then we must leave the rest to God.

Jerry Hayner

❖ ❖

6

Faith soars to heights and sees great things, hard tasks that require terrible toil, and yet does not become tired and quit; faith keeps at it and will not for any reason stop till it has done or died. God seems to delight in such souls. He stands by such dreamers and doers.

Kinley McMillan

❖ ❖

When life gets whittled down, faith doesn't. It begins by trusting God, and it ends the same way. It says, "God is worthy of my trust, no matter what!"

Gary C. Redding

7

❖ ❖

The faith pictured in the Bible is not passive; it's active, adventurous, and at times daring. Our confidence, however, comes not from the strength of our own abilities or resources but from the strength of the God we've come to believe in. God can be trusted!

❖ ❖

Faith is confidence. The Christian life is lived on the basis of the utter trustworthiness of God. Whatever happens, we are confident in him. Whatever changes, we are confident in him.

John N. Gladstone

❖ ❖

Faith is trusting God in the dark. His promises were made for dark hours.

❖ ❖

Faith endures because it is not alone. We slip our hands in the hand of God.

Roger Lovette

❖ ❖

A person should not have to carry his faith. His faith should carry him. Faith will not stop temptation, but it will stop you from yielding. Faith will not hold back trouble, but it will get you through it.

Willis E. Dewberry

❖ REFLECTION ❖

At what times or in what situations are you most prone to doubt God's love or God's promises? Memorize one of the selections of Scripture at the beginning of this chapter. Let God's Word encourage you to a deeper trust in the Lord.

❖ ❖

The best day we are living in could be the best day there has ever been. It depends on whether or not we will have the kind of faith in the goodness and the presence of God to believe that we can do something with this day. It depends not on the time we live in but on the faith we live. The God who led the people of Israel out of Egypt to the Promised Land is the God who can do the same thing for us—lead us out of the Egypt of our despair into the joy of abundant life. God will help us if we're not afraid to try.

Hugh Litchfield

❖ ❖

How great is *your* God? Is he great enough to wrap his love around you, to stand beside you, and to see you through any crisis—even though all others forsake you, even though hell itself should set itself against you? Is your God great enough to stoop to your weakness, to deal with your perverseness, to bind up your wounds, to wipe the tears from your eyes, to put his hand in your hand, his shoulder beside your shoulder—and walk you through anything and everything that life requires of you? These days demand great living, and great living depends on faith in a great God. "The Lord is a great God"—greater indeed than you and I have any capacity to understand!

Wallace Alston

9

❖ ❖

The way to increase faith is to act on the faith one has.

Arthur W. Walker Jr.

❖ ❖

Some Christians are under the impression that doubt is something bad, something to be avoided at all costs. Some of us have been scolded because we have gone through times when we have questioned God or his goodness. The truth is that doubt can be an ally of faith. We emerge from times of honest doubt with strengthened faith.

❧ ❧

We think of Gideon as one of the great heroes of the Bible—and rightly so. Yet Gideon is not at all a hero when we first meet him in the Bible. Instead he is the patron saint of all doubters. Uncertain about his faith and skeptical of God's goodness and power, Gideon complains, "Where are all his wondrous works which our fathers told us of, saying, 'Did not the Lord bring us up from Egypt?' But now the Lord has cast us off." Hardly a hero! What made the difference between Gideon the doubter and Gideon the man of God? The answer is prayer. Gideon opened his heart in the presence of the Lord and candidly stated his doubt.

Lowell M. Atkinson

❧ ❧

God plays hide-and-seek—now we glimpse him, now he is gone. We see him in moments of insight, but lose him in the routine task. We see him in retrospect, but we cannot discern him in his present ways. Sometimes we cry in glad gratitude, "The Lord is my shepherd"; sometimes we cry in agony, "Oh, that I knew where I could find him!" He does not leave us in doubt long enough to destroy our faith, nor in faith long enough to destroy our doubt!

George Buttrick, The Pulpit

❖ ❖

For my part, I have settled it with myself that without running away from doubts and questionings I am always going to put the greater emphasis on my faith. I am always going to put my doubts in the dock first. I am going to doubt doubt before I doubt faith. When it comes to an issue, I am going deliberately and consciously to trust my belief, my faith, that something deep within me that affirms God, that says yes to the God revealed in the New Testament, and seek to direct my life accordingly.

Herbert H. Farmer

❖ ❖

The worst fear is caused not by storms or the possibility of drowning but by forgetting what God has done and promises to do. The places where the Church of Jesus Christ is growing larger and stronger today are paradoxically those places where it is unsafe and uncertain—those places where the people of God *must* remember.

Carol M. Norén

❖ ❖

❧ PRAYER ❧

Almighty God, we come to you in our weakness and seek your strength. Though we speak words of trust so confidently on Sunday, we sometimes doubt those words in the trials and pressures that come the rest of the week. Thank you that we can rest completely in your faithful character and in your faithful promises. Give us the courage to trust you fully. Amen.

Douglas Connelly

"CLEANSE ME"
confession

❖ ❖

Have mercy on me, O God,
according to your steadfast love;
according to your abundant mercy
blot out my transgressions.
Wash me thoroughly from my iniquity,
and cleanse me from my sin.

PSALM 51:1-2

If we say that we have no sin, we deceive ourselves, and
the truth is not in us. If we confess our sins, he who is
faithful and just will forgive us our sins and cleanse us
from all unrighteousness.

1 JOHN 1:8-9

❖ ❖

*None of us likes to face up to what we've done wrong—especially
when we have to admit it to God. God doesn't treat sin lightly,
and we know it. Sin is whatever separates us from God—actions
or attitudes that create barriers in our relationship. We can try
to make excuses for our sin, but excuses never lead to forgiveness.
Cleansing comes only through confession.*

*When we confess, we tell God exactly what we have done and
we accept full responsibility for it. What's so amazing is that when*

we fully confess our sin, God freely forgives us. We find restoration by running to the very person we offended most deeply and telling him the truth.

❧ ❧

When we stand in the very presence of God, we know we are sinners and cannot help ourselves. We can give nothing to God to atone for sin. It is impossible to live good enough to make up for even one of our failures. We can offer no sacrifice, no gift, that will bring us back into relation with God. Our only hope is to make confession of our sin and receive God's forgiveness. Confession is more than simply the recognition of sin. It is more than regret that we have been caught. Confession is admission of sin, and the commitment that, with the help of God, we will refrain from such sin from this time forward. Confession is closely tied to repentance. This means a total change of direction, a change from pleasing self to pleasing God. We desire that God's will be done in our lives. Confession is vital, and we have the promise that when we confess, God is ready to forgive and to restore us to a fresh relationship with him.

Clayton K. Harrop

❧ ❧

To sin no more is the highest repentance.

Martin Luther

❧ ❧

In our better moments we acknowledge that we are guilty of sin and that we fail God. Much of the time, however, we may not be aware of personal sin. We look around us and see the failures in the lives of others, and we rejoice that we are not guilty of the terrible things they do. This can be dangerous because it leads us to think that we are all right and our lives are pleasing to God. But when we feel most comfortable about our lives, we are farthest away from God.

Clayton K. Harrop

❦ ❦

At times our personal and public failures are heavy on our souls before God. Leave them behind by asking for God's forgiveness and believing that God does forgive. "As the heavens are high above the earth, so great is his mercy toward them that fear him. As far as the east is from the west, so far has he removed our transgressions from us." Ask him to do it and then believe and forget them once and for all. Many of us go prowling around behind God's back, uncovering the sins that are buried there.

M.K.W. Heicher

❦   REFLECTION   ❦

What failures have you gone prowling around behind God's back to uncover? What steps can you take to remind yourself of God's promise of cleansing so you can be set free from the memory of those sins?

❦ ❦

In the hour of a person's deepest need, it is not the vision of new horizons for which his soul cries out. It is not for a new and nobler idea of life and service that he yearns with all the intensity of his being. It is for the cleansing power of the living God to sweep right down to the depths of his nature—to be purged and purified, as he has never been before.

D. P. Thomson

❧ ❧

To repent is not to speak great words but to lament to God from the heart our sorrow about ourselves. We tell God particular things that we have thought, said, and done—things we know are not right before him and by which it becomes clear to us that we have a disobedient heart. Repentance is the acknowledgment of our sin before God, who has done so many good things for us and whom we have repaid with such unthankfulness. That is why repentance necessarily flows into a prayer for forgiveness of sins and for a heart obedient to God.

18

❧ ❧

It is just at the moment that we confess our failings that we are most fully conscious of God's help.

Donald Anderson

❧ ❧

Once we have faced our failures openly and honestly before God and before those we have offended, we find a new sense of humility and grace flowing from us to the people who have hurt us. We are slower to judge and quicker to forgive. We listen to the confessions of others not with smug condemnation but with hearts willing to forgive.

❧ ❧

Forgiven people know best how to love. The more we realize how much Jesus has forgiven each of us, the more we are motivated to love God and other people in tangible ways.

Ron E. Blankenship

19

❧ ❧

"Judge not, that you not be judged." In judging other people we automatically set standards by which the world will most certainly judge us, and in doing so we make our critical censure a boomerang. Psychologists tells us that we ourselves offend at the very points for which we criticize others because the fault we find most irritating in another person is usually the fault we most hate in ourselves but which we have not the courage to face.

Leonard Griffith

❧ ❧

Mature Christians who hear confessions must be a forgiving community whose ears are open to hear and to help, but whose mouths are forever sealed thereafter.

James Earl Massey

❧ PRAYER ❧

O God of mercy and judgment, we acknowledge that we have fallen short. We have deceived ourselves and others so that we might be excused. We confess that we have not felt the need to confess because we have measured our merit by those around us. We have closed our eyes to the needs of others. We have judged them severely and ourselves easily. We have called our sin by kinder names, and we have chosen the wrong when we have known the right. Create in us a clean heart, O God, and renew a right spirit within us.

Chester E. Hodgson

―――――――

following jesus

❦ ❦

"Truly I tell you, there is no one who has left house or brothers or sisters or mother or father or children or fields, for my sake and for the sake of the good news, who will not receive a hundredfold now in this age—houses, brothers and sisters, mothers and children, and fields, with persecutions and in the age to come eternal life."

JESUS IN MARK 10:29-30

❖ ❖

The Christian life is an adventure. Jesus doesn't ask us to join a new organization; he calls us to a life of commitment. Following Jesus is not a hobby or a passing interest. Following Jesus means giving him priority over everything and everyone else.

Some people aren't very interested in following Jesus. They think it will be too difficult or too oppressive, or that they will have to give up too much. They don't realize that it is when we willingly submit to Jesus as Lord that we gain everything of true value. We may lose the world but we gain our own soul. Not everyone has the courage to follow Jesus fully. Those who do make the commitment find themselves on fire with a passionate love for Jesus.

❖ ❖

Has someone seen Jesus in you today?

❖ ❖

A real Christian is an odd number. He feels supreme love for one whom he has never seen. He talks familiarly every day to someone he cannot see. He expects to go to heaven on the virtue of someone else. He empties himself in order that he might be full. He admits he is wrong so he can be declared right. He goes down in order to get up. He is strongest when he is poorest and happiest when he feels worst. He dies so he can live, forsakes in order to have, gives away so he can keep, sees the invisible, hears the inaudible, and knows things that surpass mere human wisdom.

A. W. Tozer

❖ ❖

The gospel is at heart quite simple. You can boil it down to a single concept. The invitation of Jesus is so clear a child can grasp it. He simply says, "Come, follow me." But the gospel is a many-faceted thing. Following Christ is the most demanding challenge you will ever take on. He also says, "Learn about me." You will spend the rest of your life doing that.

Alton H. McEachern

❖ ❖

There are a great many things which the Lord will put up with in the human heart; but there is one thing he will not put up with—second place.

John Ruskin

❧ REFLECTION ❧

When we love someone, we express that love. How do you express your love and devotion to Jesus? If someone were to watch closely the way you live, what priority would they say Jesus has in your life?

❧ ❧

25

The great New Testament confession of faith is that Jesus Christ is Lord. This is the creed, this is the belief, for which Christians in the early days were prepared to die and did die. This was the creed which brought them into head-on collision with the Roman Empire. The basic creed of the Roman Empire was, "Caesar is Lord." The Emperor was regarded as a god in whom the deity, the genius, the spirit of Rome was incarnated. There came a time when every Roman citizen had once a year to burn his pinch of incense to the godhead of the emperor and say, "Caesar is Lord." It was precisely this that the Christians would never do. For them Jesus Christ was Lord, and they would give the title *Lord* to no man; and for that reason they were looked on as dangerous and disaffected citizens, to be persecuted to the death.

William Barclay

❧ ❧

Being a fully committed follower of Christ doesn't mean that life is easy. You and I may have to face difficult situations because of our commitment to Jesus. But we are willing to face those challenges because we love Jesus so much.

❧ ☙

Two inflexible rules of following Jesus: First, if you follow Jesus, there will come a day, somewhere, sometime, when Jesus will call you to do something that will require setting aside something really meaningful and very dear. Jesus will smack you right between the eyes with something—some ministry to perform, some job to do—and it will become crystal clear to you that you cannot both obey him and keep your fists closed tightly around that thing that is so dear to you. That's the first rule of the road with Jesus. The other is that unless you give that thing away, you will never know what it is really like to live. Jesus' rule is absolute: unless you lay down your life you lose it; but if you lay it down, then you get it back again, renewed and resurrected. Are you prepared to lighten your load? When Jesus calls you and says, "Follow me here," are you prepared to lay down all the stuff you're trying to carry, all the stuff you've crammed into your suitcases and closets and garages, all the stuff you've tucked away inside your soul, all the things about your life that you think define you—are you prepared to lay them down to follow Jesus?

Richard B. Vinson

❧ ☙

26

Give me the love that leads the way,
The faith that nothing can dismay,
The hope no disappointments tire,
The passion that will burn like fire.
Let me not sink to be a clod;
Make me Thy fuel, Flame of God.

Amy Carmichael

❖ PRAYER ❖

Lord Jesus, give us the courage to respond to your call and to live in such a way that our love for you is obvious to those around us. Show us every day how we can more fully follow you. Burn in our hearts, Flame of God. Amen.

Douglas Connelly

27

"FORGIVE AS
THE LORD FORGIVES YOU"

forgiveness

❧ ❧

Happy are those whose transgressions are forgiven,
whose sin is covered.

PSALM 32:1

Be kind to one another, tenderhearted, forgiving one
another, as God in Christ has forgiven you.

EPHESIANS 4:32

"Whenever you stand praying, forgive, if you have anything against anyone; so that your Father in heaven
may also forgive you your trespasses."

JESUS IN MARK 11:25

❧ ❧

*Jesus' followers asked him one day how often they should forgive
someone who deliberately sins against them. The disciples thought
they were generous in offering to forgive another person seven times.
Jesus' response was stunning. He said that we are to forgive seventy
times seven. In other words, don't keep track of forgiveness. There's
no limit, no end, no account to use up.*

Forgiveness is hard work. We don't just forget sin, we forgive sin. That means we bear the pain and the price of someone else's deliberate wrong against us—and we do it willingly. The only reason Jesus could make such an outrageous demand of us is because he was willing to pay the ultimate price to provide forgiveness to us.

❦ ❦

Forgiveness is the wonder of being trusted again by God in the place where I disgraced him.

Rita F. Snowden

30

❦ ❦

A saintly African Christian once told a congregation that as he was climbing the hill to the meeting, he heard steps behind him. He turned and saw a man carrying a very heavy load on his back up the hill. He was full of sympathy for the man and spoke to him. Then he noticed that the man's hands were scarred and he realized that it was Jesus. He said to him, "Lord, are you carrying the world's sins up the hill?" "No," said Jesus, "not the world's sins, just yours!" As that African simply told the vision God had just given him, the peoples' hearts and his heart were broken as they saw their sins. Our hearts need to be broken, too, and only when they are shall we be willing for the confessions, the apologies, the reconciliation, and the restitution that are involved in a true repentance of sin.

Roy and Revel Hession

❦ ❦

We cannot cope until we can accept ourselves, and we cannot accept ourselves until we sense that we are forgiven—radically forgiven. Men and women, God has covered the past with his limitless grace. He has already wiped out our transgressions as the dawn rises on a new day.

❖ ❖

Some people all through Jesus' ministry were filled with hatred and tried to stop Jesus. Why? Because he gave too much love and forgave too many people for their sins.

Ron E. Blankenship

❖ ❖

It cost God something to forgive us; it cost him the cross.

Charles Gerlinger

❖ ❖

Forgiving the unforgivable is hard. So was the cross: hard words, hard wood, hard nails.

William S. Stoddard

❖ ❖

People who have experienced the forgiveness of God make great forgivers! The only appropriate response to God's forgiveness is to forgive those who have hurt us.

❖ ❖

Jesus said that unless we are willing to forgive others, God will not be willing to forgive us. Why does God say that the practice of forgiveness is a condition for receiving it? Forgiveness is the only proper response to the forgiveness we have already received. It was a very difficult thing for God to forgive us. It was difficult because God took sin seriously. That meant he had to step into human history and make that long shameful journey all the way to the cross. The forgiveness we want is the forgiveness we must give. If we fail to reach out in love and mercy to others, how can we possibly expect that God is going to reach out with his forgiveness to us?

Arthur McPhee

32

❖ ❖

The only petition in the Lord's Prayer that has a condition attached is the one about forgiveness. God will not forgive us if we maintain an unforgiving attitude toward others.

❖ ❖

The truest measure of your Christian maturity is not the actions of your life but your attitude toward sinners who have found their way back into the Father's house. Are you critical or compassionate? That is the key. Jesus made it clear that we can be forgiven only as we forgive.

❖ ❖

❖ REFLECTION ❖

Think about the people in your past who have wounded you. Those are the people God calls you to forgive. Regardless of their response to you, you can be released from the bitterness and bondage of an unforgiving heart.

❖ ❖

God's Forgiveness
- God forgives immediately.
- God forgives fully.
- God forgives willingly.
- God forgets as well as forgives: "I will remember their sins no more forever."

33

❖ ❖

Among all the troubles, problems, and needs that a congregation brings with them to church, one above all others is ever present: the need for forgiveness. Where even two or three are gathered together, there will you find this strange need for forgiveness.

Robert E. Luccock

❖ ❖

True forgiveness always requires restoration, and that is why true forgiveness is so difficult.

Robert U. Ferguson

❖ ❖

❧ PRAYER ❧

Father, as we pray this prayer of forgiveness, we know that by the giving of your Son for the forgiveness of our sins, they are forgiven. As we pray this prayer, we cannot help but be humbled and conscious of your great love at work in our lives. Not only do we feel humbled, but we also feel strengthened, empowered, and ready to face the challenges of a new day.

James R. Rosenburg

"HOLY AND DEARLY LOVED"

Grace

❧ ❧

The Lord, the Lord,
a God merciful and gracious, slow to anger,
and abounding in steadfast love and faithfulness.

EXODUS 34:6

But let all who take refuge in you rejoice;
let them ever sing for joy. . . .
For you bless the righteous, O Lord;
you cover them with favor as with a shield.

PSALM 5:11A, 12

Let us therefore approach the throne of grace with
boldness, so that we may receive mercy and find grace
to help in time of need.

HEBREWS 4:16

❖ ❖

*No one deserves grace—that's why it's grace! Grace is undeserved
kindness. It's a patient mother with a moody child; it's an understanding teacher with a daydreaming student; it's a father wel-
coming home the runaway son who squandered his inheritance
and ended up in a pigpen.*

Our God is a gracious God—an extravagant, joyful giver. He has an inexhaustible supply of good gifts—gifts available to anyone and everyone who will receive them. That's all we have to do with grace. We don't have to earn it or deserve it or live up to a certain standard to get it. All we must do with what grace offers is receive it.

❖ ❖

The only response to grace is gratitude.

Gary D. Stratman

38

❖ ❖

One of the hardest lessons we have to learn from Christ is that our most important need is not to love and to forgive but to be loved and to be forgiven. We need to recognize that we live in dependence on God's graciousness to us. Our pride needs to be broken on the love of God as seen in Christ's dying on a cross for us. Humbled by God's undeserved love for us, we are readied to share that love with others.

Culbert S. Cartwright

❖ ❖

Think how a little child accepts a gift—openly, gladly, and unhindered by any reserve or reluctance. That is how we should accept the grace of God.

Robert J. McCracken

❖ ❖

Paul says, "My God shall supply all your needs." The Amplified Bible reads, "And my God will liberally supply and fill to the full every need." Someone has said that God has four accounts that are mentioned in Scripture. There are the riches of his goodness (Romans 2:4), the riches of his wisdom (Romans 11:33), the riches of his grace (Ephesians 1:7), and the riches of his glory (Ephesians 1:18). It is out of the last account that God will supply all of our needs, and the implication is that this source is incomparable, infinite, and inexhaustible.

Brian Harbour

᯾ REFLECTION ᯾   39

Think about how you have responded in the last twenty-four hours to God's good gifts to you. How many gifts can you name or write down? Now use your creative imagination to express your gratitude—through prayer or through a song or through an unexpected act of grace toward another person.

᯾ ᯾

What we were: nobodies, rejected.
What we are: God's own people, precious.
What we can be: witnesses of God's marvelous grace.

᯾ ᯾

We are saved by grace, not by our best and highest ethical striving. We don't win God's acceptance by being good. I bring empty hands to God and I say to him, "I have nothing to bring to you. I wish I had full hands. I would like to bring you many moral virtues." God looks at me and says a most wonderful thing: "Your empty hands are enough. If you had all the moral wealth in the world, you couldn't buy my salvation. It is of grace. It is a gift."

❧ ❧

Jesus pictured God's grace as the payment of an enormous debt that human beings owed God, a debt that we could never repay. God could have condemned us, but instead he took the obligation of the debt on himself. God paid our debt through Jesus' sacrifice on the cross. God fully, freely, incredibly paid the debt we owed— and God is now eager to forgive.

❧ ❧

"Cheap grace" is the preaching of forgiveness without requiring repentance; the offering of baptism, Communion, or marriage without requiring preparation, discipline, promises, or demands; religious privilege without responsibility; glibly confessing our sins without having a sincere contrite heart, without having the slightest intention of change on our part or any real resolution at all to do better in our life. Cheap grace is grace without discipleship, grace without the cross, grace without sacrifice, grace without Jesus in our lives.

Murray H. Voth

❧ ❧

The gospel message of the Christian faith is different from the gospel of hard work. Jesus said that we are not forgiven and redeemed by what we do but by whether or not we are willing to accept the forgiveness already offered, to allow it into the very center of our being.

Rick Brand

❖ ❖

The most important thing we can give our children is a sense of grace. I didn't earn it, possess it, build it myself. The very fabric of the universe is a gift.

Gary D. Stratman

41

❖ ❖

Amazing grace! how sweet the sound,
That saved a wretch like me!
I once was lost, but now am found,
Was blind, but now I see.
Through many dangers, toils and snares,
I have already come;
'Tis grace hath brought me safe thus far,
And grace will lead me home.

John Newton

❖ ❖

❧ PRAYER ❧

We've had a warped view of you, God. Too often we've pictured you sitting in heaven with a club, waiting to punish us. In reality you are a gracious Father, waiting for a wandering child to return. So we turn to you today with our empty hands, knowing that you will fill them with good gifts. We have nothing to offer you—except our gratitude. Amen.

Douglas Connelly

"WHY HAVE YOU FORSAKEN ME?"

suffering

❦ ❦

Be gracious to me, O Lord, for I am in distress;
my eye wastes away from grief,
my soul and my body also.
For my life is spent with sorrow,
and my years with sighing;
my strength fails because of my misery,
and my bones waste away.

PSALM 31:9-10

45
—

I consider that the sufferings of this present time are
not worth comparing with the glory about to be
revealed to us.

ROMANS 8:18

❖ ❖

The contributors to The Minister's Manual *have not just been
preachers; they have also been pastors. Most of them have spent
many years caring for a congregation of people. Along the way they
have learned a lot about suffering. These pastor-friends do not
speak to us from the protection of a comfortable office. They speak
from the pain of standing with people at a hospital bed or outside
a divorce courtroom or next to a fresh grave. You won't find easy*

answers in these selections. ~~Easy answers never help~~. What you will find is quiet comfort for your hurting heart.

❦ ❦

Being flat on your back puts you in a good position to look up.

❦ ❦

The myth that must be rejected, if we are to experience the nearness of God, is the myth that we are exempted by our faith from ever being broken or crushed. Despite cultural denial and false teaching, the Scripture is clear: the rain falls on the just and the unjust. Believers and nonbelievers both can and do receive the good things in life. Both the unjust and the just also know the sting of pain, disappointment, and loss. The question that plagues us is not *Is there suffering?* but *Why me and mine?* It was Jesus who cried out, "My God, my God, why have you forsaken me?" As Donald McCullough graphically paraphrases it, "My God, where in the hell are you when I need you?"

Gary D. Stratman

❦ ❦

The only guarantee Christians have is that tough times will come. If you haven't already, you will eventually go through the fire.

Gary C. Redding

❦ ❦

You are not responsible for the way things are in this world. You are responsible for what you do with the way things are. If you are not happy, it's not because of the life that has been given to you. It's because of what you've done with the life that has been given to you. The past may explain you, but it doesn't excuse you.

Mark Trotter

❧ REFLECTION ❧

When have you blamed your bad attitude or wrong behavior on some past experience or injustice? Consider what your life might be like if you were willing to give that past hurt over to God.

47

❧ ❧

"Time heals all wounds." I've heard it all my life, as you have, but it isn't so. Time does *not* heal all wounds. More than time is needed to heal many of our wounds. Jesus heals those deep wounds—if we are willing to be healed.

David Albert Farmer

❧ ❧

Since we do not know what is best, we cannot even pray for the removal of our troubles.

Ansley C. Moore

❧ ❧

Is the Christian faith good only for the happy times? The easy times? The uncomplicated times? Or is it relevant and support-ive for the tough times, the times of adversity and reverses and unexplained tragedies? Do we as Christians witness to our faith and the adequacy of God's grace when we lose our job? Or when we see our investments melting away? Or when sickness or be-reavement come? Or when our children are proving to be a dis-appointment? Or when our highest hopes turn to heartaches? Do we as the redeemed of the Lord demonstrate that no per-manent disaster can ever come to a person whose faith is in Jesus? The Christian, of course, is just as sensitive to pain or sorrow or setbacks as others. But by personalizing the promises of God, he says to the world, or to his corner of it, that God's grace is truly sufficient and that through the presence and power of his God, he will see it through victoriously.

William Fisher

❧ ❧

The most glorious result of the humanity of Jesus is that he is able to understand what we are going through. When you get tired and don't think you can go on, he understands. When you are treated unfairly by others, he understands. When those whom you love most dearly let you down, he understands. When your parents don't understand and your brothers make fun of you, he understands. When you are left out and ignored, he understands. When your best laid plans are sabotaged by the jealousy and envy of others, he understands. When you stand at the tomb of one whom you loved with all your heart and cry, "Why did it have to happen?" he understands.

Brian L. Harbour

❦ ❦

The power of God does not lie in protecting you from failure, frustration, tragedy, or death; the power of God lies in taking the worst life can do to us and transforming it into a new, deeper, and more profound reality.

James W. Crawford

❦ ❦

49

The writers of Scripture never try to explain human suffering. Instead they ask one simple question: Are you willing to trust God even in the darkness? God promises that he will never abandon us in our pain. Whatever we experience, he experiences with us.

❦ ❦

There is good news in the discovery that as we suffer, *God suffers with us.* This is not good news just because misery loves company. Misery does not love company that well. There is great spiritual healing in the companionship of a God who shares our deepest grief, our sharpest pain, our darkest despair. We discover that God does not willingly afflict us or complacently stand by as a spectator. Whatever we suffer, he suffers with us.

Robert E. Luccock

❦ ❦

God whispers to us in our pleasures, speaks to us in our conscience, but shouts to us in our pains.

C. S. Lewis

❦ ❦

What a friend we have in Jesus,
All our sins and griefs to bear!
What a privilege to carry
Everything to God in prayer!
O what peace we often forfeit,
O, what needless pain we bear,
All because we do not carry
Everything to God in prayer!

Joseph Scriven

50

❦ PRAYER ❦

Healing and comforting God, Great Physician, God of tender heart and abiding comfort, who in Christ has suffered for all who suffer, we pray today for all who are suffering in mind and in spirit, and whose hearts are broken. May your healing and reclaiming presence encircle them with hope and wholeness. Grant us the humility and courage to suffer with you and the blessing to be comforters with you.

William M. Johnson

"HOW WIDE AND
LONG AND HIGH AND DEEP"

god's love

❧ ❧

"I have loved you with an everlasting love; therefore I have continued my faithfulness to you."

JEREMIAH 31:3

God is love, and those who abide in love abide in God, and God abides in them.

1 JOHN 4:16

❖ ❖

"God is love" is one of the most soul-stirring statements in the Bible. God expresses love in everything he says and does. God's love is not the soft love of an indulgent grandparent; it's a holy, pure, and at times severe love that will go to any extreme to rescue and provide for those who are loved. God's love could allow Jesus to go to the cross, knowing that throngs of human beings would be reconciled to God because of Jesus' sacrifice. Whatever happens to us as Christians is ultimately a demonstration of what James Packer calls God's "cosmic generosity."

❖ ❖

God's love is unconditional. He did not love me under certain conditions; he did not wait until I merited love. Rather, his love came to me while I was yet a sinner.

Daniel C. Whitaker

❧ ☙

God's love is the love that will not let us go, will not let us down, and will not let us off.

Ganse Little

❧ ☙

God is a God of love. God loves the world so much that he gave himself in the person of Jesus, his only Son. Love is the mystery, the greatest mystery. Believe in the mystery of the love of God. You'll still have tears, and in the darkness of night you'll sometimes tremble with the same old fears. But always there will come the assurance that, in a way no one can ever understand, God cares. God loves those who put their trust in Jesus. God loves those who repent of their sins and believe in Jesus. He loves them so much that he takes the precious blood of Jesus and washes all their sins away.

Joel Nederhood

❧ ☙

❖ REFLECTION ❖

When do you tend to doubt God's love for you? As you read again the Scripture passages and selections that begin this chapter, allow yourself to feel your Father's warm embrace. Even if you feel far from God, he is ready and anxious to receive you.

❖ ❖

God pursues us like a persistent mother searching for a lost child, like a compassionate baker seeking out the starving in order to give them bread, like a thoughtful clown looking for a hospital ward in which to make sad people laugh. We cannot get away from God.

Welton Gaddy

❖ ❖

Even when we cannot see why or how God is working for good in our lives, we can know that God's love is in and behind every event. We can rest—and rejoice—in God's great love, even when it seems that life has taken a wrong turn.

❖ ❖

God never makes false promises, telling you that he'll take away all your problems if you come to him. He does promise you his peace, which will calm your troubled, resistant heart. He promises you his strength to meet the difficulties of day-in, day-out

55

existence. He says, "Do you take me at my word? Will you experience all the promises I have for you? My love is total. It's complete. It's lasting. My love will never fail you."

John A Huffman Jr.

❧ ❧

The same God who has loved us throughout history loves you today. When life fluctuates to the low extreme, God loves you. When moments of hurt and insecurity come, remember that God loves you. When no one seems to care about you, remember that God loves you. When friends and family let you down, God loves you. When you are disappointed, frustrated, facing tragedy, death, and defeat, when you have cried until your tears have dried up, remember that God loves you and you are not alone. But above all, when you need a savior, remember that God loves you so much that he sent his Son to save you.

W. Matt Tomlin

56

❧ ❧

Many of the great hymns of the faith resonate with the love of God. Charles Wesley's "And Can It Be That I Should Gain" expresses the wonder and awe we experience when we catch a glimpse of the depth of God's love for us.

❧ ❧

He left his Father's throne above,
So free, so infinite his grace;
Emptied himself of all but love,
And bled for Adam's helpless race;
'Tis mercy all, immense and free;
For, O my God, it found out me.
Amazing love! how can it be
That thou, my God, shouldst die for me.

Charles Wesley

❧ ☙

God's love is not weak and sentimental; his love is strong enough   57
to stand aside and let us suffer the consequences of our sins.

Earl Davis

❧ ☙

The love of God bears things that others think unbearable, believes things that others think questionable, hopes when others have yielded to despair, and endures when others have fallen away. Such love turns fear to faith.

Albert J. D. Walsh

❧ ☙

❧ PRAYER ❧

Loving Father, what a comfort it is to sense your heart of love for us. Even when we are far from you, you set your affection on us and determine to make us your own dear children. Help us to bask each day in the warmth of your goodness and delight in us. Amen.

Douglas Connelly

"LISTEN TO ME, O GOD"

prayer

❖ ❖

For God alone my soul waits in silence;
from him comes my salvation.
He alone is my rock and my salvation, my fortress;
I shall never be shaken.

PSALM 62:1-2

Do not worry about anything, but in everything by
prayer and supplication with thanksgiving let your re-
quests be made known to God. And the peace of God,
which surpasses all understanding, will guard your
hearts and your minds in Christ Jesus.

PHILIPPIANS 4:6-7

❖ ❖

*A friend of mine said something recently that I've heard many
times. He said, "I believe in the power of prayer." For some reason,
his words lodged in my mind for a long time, and the more I
thought about what he said, the more I disagreed with him. There
is no power in prayer! Prayer is an admission of powerlessness. The
power resides in the person to whom we pray. Prayer is more than*

*words; it is getting off our knees knowing that we have tapped into
the resources of a God of power and grace.*

❖ ❖

You can't simply go to lectures on prayer or read books about
it. You have to do it.

Theodore Parker Ferris

❖ ❖

Whatever the invading anxiety is in your life, you can go up before God and spread it out before him. When blessing comes,
you can thank God. When burdens come, you can seek God's
assistance. When you have failed, you can ask for God's forgiveness. When you have succeeded, you can praise God for his help.
When you don't know what to do, you can ask God for his guidance. You can pray to God about everything.

Brian Harbour

❖ ❖

Let's face the fact that many of us pray only when we are in trouble. We seek God's help only when our own strength has entirely
failed. For this reason, many of our biggest discoveries concern-
ing God have come when we have been desperately in need and
when there has been no one else to whom we could go. There
are countless thousands of men and women all over the world

who could say that they never knew how loving and how dependable God was until they were in trouble.

J. H. Jowett

❖ ❖

Prayer is both a great mystery and a wonderful simplicity. We come to God as a child comes to a loving, attentive parent, but when we get there, we find ourselves in conversation with the God who rules over all creation in majesty and power. We are welcomed into God's presence not to wait nervously for a spare moment of his time but to be caught up in his loving embrace.

63

❖ ❖

Here we are at the heart of prayer. The God whom you meet is your heavenly Father. Therefore, as his child, bring all your problems, all your desires, all your longings to him and ask him to decide what is your deepest need. In his infinite wisdom, he will give you that which will be a blessing, not an evil, to you.

John Sutherland Bonnell

❖ ❖

"Draw near to God, and he will draw near to you" (James 4:8). That is the greatest Word in the Bible about prayer—that through prayer we are able to draw near to God and experience a rich fellowship with him. Trace Christian history and you will find the same key. Whenever there has been a great spiritual awakening, whenever there has been a mighty movement of the people of God, that awakening and that movement can be traced back to Christians on their knees before God in prayer.

Brian Harbour

❖ REFLECTION ❖

Do you pray only in an emergency or is prayer a continuing conversation with God? The way to begin a life of prayer is to carve out just five minutes every day to quiet yourself before God. Tell him your concerns, thank him for his provision, express your gratitude for his goodness, listen for his response of love. As you get to know God, your time with him will become more of a priority.

64
—

❖ ❖

Prayer was a priority for Jesus. It came first before job, family, friends, responsibilities. His procedure was simple: He made time to pray. He did not try to find time to pray. If we pray when we find the time, we'll never pray! There's no time to be found! Jesus made time for prayer. He was intentional and disciplined in his prayer life. Jesus made time, found a quiet place, and there he prayed. Then he was ready to face the demands of the new day.

Craig A. Loscalzo

❖ ❖

Satan dreads nothing but prayer. Because he fears nothing from prayerless studies, prayerless work, and prayerless religion, his one concern is to keep the saints from praying. He laughs at our toil and mocks our wisdom, but he trembles when we pray.

Samuel Chadwick

❖ ❖

For Jesus and the prophets, prayer was not an escape but an empowerment. It was not the attempt to find a hiding place but the attempt to find that hidden spring welling up within to enable them to do the will of God. Prayer was power. Prayer is power to change people, to withstand the temptation to an easy life, to see clearly, and to act rightly.

William Jackson Jarman

65

❖ ❖

We sometimes think that prayer is designed to twist God's arm. It isn't. Prayer won't change God, or our circumstances. When I pray humbly and honestly, prayer changes me. My will is gradually shaped to fit the Father's will.

❖ ❖

People of prayer must knock and knock—sometimes with bleeding knuckles in the dark.

George A. Buttrick

❖ ❖

There is real peril in answered prayer. To pray for God's will in your life is to risk being called to a duty that becomes the compelling will of God.

Hoover Rupert

❖ ❖

There are some things that prayer cannot do. Prayer will not reverse some of the circumstances in our lives. Prayer will not change a bad grade. Prayer will not weave a shield around us so as to protect us from hardship, harm, and disappointment. Prayer will not reverse the course of gravity. Because, you see, there are just some things that prayer cannot change, no matter how hard we pray. What *can* prayer change? Prayer can change us so that we can better handle the circumstances of life. Prayer will not reverse a hard circumstance in our life, no matter how difficult that circumstance is and how painful it has been for us. No matter how hard we might pray, prayer will not make life like it once was. But prayer can give to us the inner faith we need to handle that circumstance wisely and well.

Joe E. Pennel Jr.

❖ ❖

Prayer *always* changes us.

John Huess

❖ ❖

❖ PRAYER ❖

Lord, we confess our reluctance to pray. It's hard to find the time, and we are so busy running our lives we forget how interested you are in us. Remind us that you are waiting to converse with us, that you enjoy our company, and that no need is outside the scope of your concern or power. Amen.

Douglas Connelly

"THE LORD BLESSES HIS PEOPLE"
Thankfulness

❧ ❧

Praise the Lord, all you nations!
Extol him, all you peoples!
For great is his steadfast love toward us,
and the faithfulness of the Lord endures forever.
Praise the Lord!

PSALM 117

Give thanks in all circumstances; for this is the will
of God in Christ Jesus for you.

1 THESSALONIANS 5:18

God is able to provide you with every blessing in
abundance.

2 CORINTHIANS 9:11

❖ ❖

*Gratitude is a flower that seems difficult to grow. Ironically, we
are least thankful when we enjoy prosperity and peace. It's in the
stubborn soil of hardship and loss that thankfulness grows best—
when the business collapses or the marriage dissolves or the diag-
nosis is bad. That's when we begin to appreciate all the good things
God has given to us.*

My wife, Karen, makes a conscious effort at times to thank God for everything she encounters in the course of her day—a car that runs well and takes her where she wants to go, a good school for our son, comfortable clothes, enjoyable meals, a glass of cold water. She also thanks God for the traffic jam that delays her on the highway, the busy demands of her job, or caring for a sick child in the evening. I've tried Karen's approach a few times. It goes pretty well—until the first traffic jam.

❦ ❦

There are three kinds of giving: grudge giving, duty giving, and thanksgiving. Grudge giving says, "I have to"; duty giving says, "I ought to"; and thanksgiving says, "I want to." The first comes from constraint, the second from a sense of obligation, and the third from a full heart.

Robert N. Rodenmayer

❦ ❦

Saying thanks is not the same as giving thanks.

Richard N. Rinker

❦ ❦

Some would say that the hardest thanksgiving is that which we make in adversity. It is hard to give thanks when you are hungry, when life hurts, while enduring pain, when bereaved; but Christians in adversity should not lose appreciation of the goodness of God. In living the thankful life, we heed the words of Paul, "Give thanks whatever happens." In joy or sorrow, in comfort or suffering, in gain or loss, in prosperity or adversity—give thanks, remembering that it is within the power of God to make all things work together for good, and that nothing can separate us from the love of Christ.

M.K.W. Heicher

⚜ ⚜

O God, our loving Father, teach us today what to be thankful for, even if at the present moment our problems, our pain, or our need might lead us to believe that we have no cause for thanksgiving. Let your Spirit open our eyes to your unfailing goodness.

71

⚜ ⚜

Count your thankfulness as a sacrament and do not take God's simple gifts for granted. Your thankfulness is a recognition of your dependence on a God of goodness and mercy.

⚜ REFLECTION ⚜

Take a few minutes for quiet thought and write down some of the good things in your life that you normally take for granted. Now express your thankfulness to God in some creative way—in a prayer, in a song, in a letter, by sharing your gratitude with someone else. How can you cultivate a spirit of gratitude on a daily basis?

⚜ ⚜

We are long on our demands, even our complaints; we are short on our thanksgivings.

Paul S. Rees

❧ ❧

Thankfulness is an attitude and emotion that needs to be and should be claimed by everyone. "It is a good thing to give thanks unto the Lord," wrote the psalmist. "From the rising of the sun to the going down of the same, the Lord's name is to be praised." Similarly, Paul writes to the Ephesians as follows: "Be filled with the Spirit . . . always and for everything giving thanks in the name of our Lord Jesus Christ to God." There is nothing more important to anyone than the achievement of a thanks-filled life. This is the first and most basic step along the pathway to a life that is filled with faith and trust and hopefulness. To give thanks "always and for everything" is to transform our daily experiences and to change and lift our lives.

Edward C. Dahl

❧ ❧

Almighty and most merciful God, you are very good to us, beyond all thought and imagination—strengthening for toil, shielding from danger, cheering in sorrow. Pardon our ingratitude, our distrust, our disobedience.

❧ ❧

Thankfulness is an essential element in our worship of God, too. When we gather as Christians, we have a delightful opportunity to join our praise with the praise of others and to express our gratitude to God in unison.

❧ ❧

How easy it is to let our religion degenerate into mere rule keeping. Our Christian service is so often characterized by joyless obedience rather than joyous thanksgiving. We methodically do what we have been told. We mindlessly do what we know we should. We mechanically keep the rules. But rarely do we move beyond thoughtless obedience to Christian gratitude. Faith is more than obedience.

Charles J. Scalise

❧ PRAYER ❧

Let us give thanks to God our Father for all his gifts so freely bestowed upon us. For the wonder of your creation, in earth and sky and sea, we thank you, Lord. For all that is gracious in the lives of men and women, revealing the image of Christ, we thank you, Lord. For our daily food and drink, our homes and families and friends, we thank you, Lord. For minds to think, and hearts to love, and hands to serve, we thank you, Lord. For health and strength to work and leisure to rest and play, we thank you, Lord. Above all, we give you thanks for the great mercies and promises given to us in Christ Jesus our Lord; to him be praise and glory, with you, O Father, and the Holy Spirit, now and forever. Amen.

The Book of Common Prayer

life

together

from the moment of birth, we find ourselves linked to other people. Our parents become our first connection, followed by siblings, grandparents, and a whole tribe of relatives. As we grow older, we learn to enjoy friends and teachers and sweethearts. In time we get married to that special person who shares our most intimate feelings and we cultivate deep relationships with a cluster of friends who walk with us through life's joys and sorrows. As Christians, we find ourselves linked to pastors and fellow congregational members, to others in the choir, and to the people in our small group Bible study. Beyond these circles are the people we work with, our neighbors, and our community at large.

The next nine chapters explore how we relate to our world and the people in it. We will look at marriage and parenting and church life and work life. We will also seek God's guidance in practical areas, such as how we spend our money and how we respond to injustice in society.

Pick a chapter that interests you. Open yourself to its wisdom and insight. What you learn may change your life—and you may change your world!

"THE TWO WILL BECOME ONE"

marriage

❖ ❖

Set me as a seal upon your heart,
as a seal upon your arm;
for love is strong as death,
passion fierce as the grave.
Its flashes are flashes of fire,
a raging flame.
Many waters cannot quench love,
neither can floods drown it.

SONG OF SOLOMON 7:6-7

"Have you not read that the one who made them at
the beginning made them male and female, and said,
'For this reason a man shall leave his father and mother
and be joined to this wife, and the two shall become
one flesh'? So they are no longer two, but one flesh.
Therefore what God has joined together, let no one
separate."

JESUS IN MATTHEW 19:4-6

❧ ❧

According to the book of Genesis, the first wedding took place in a
luxuriant garden. It was a very simple affair—a beautiful bride,

a nervous groom, and a proud Father. But that first marriage union became the pattern for hundreds of generations of human beings. Marriage is one of the foundational structures that God established and designed for the purpose of preserving and protecting human society.

Christians have always championed the sanctity of marriage. Pastors and church leaders speak often about why marriage is important and how we as Christians can keep the spark of joy and romance alive in our marriages. A growing, fulfilling marriage doesn't just happen; it takes joyful commitment every day.

~ ~

80
—

A devoted love makes it easy for a wife to be true to her husband or a husband to his wife. There is a wonderful purifying power in love. Love is a mighty transforming influence.

~ ~

Love must be renewed daily. Life cannot be lived on a past experience if love is to be strong and fresh. Love is to be an ever new experience with us. Husband and wife must gather new supplies of love and patience and thoughtfulness every day.

~ ~

To contemplate intimacy with another person at the level suggested by marriage is a fearful step, too fearful for some to take. It requires a level of self-surrender that is awesome. For two to become one necessitates a death of self. To covenant with another in this way allows neither to speak an "I will" for self alone. Each speaks also for the other.

E. Glenn Hinson

❧ ☙

The Arithmetic of Marriage

    1. There is one (Genesis 2:18–20).

    2. There are two (Genesis 2:21–22).

    3. The two are one (Genesis 2:23–24).

81

❧ ☙

The first rush of romance and affection that newly married couples experience gradually evolves into the hard work of renewing intimacy and love through difficult days, changing career paths, and the growth of a family. Wise words help make the transition smoother.

❧ ☙

Every couple who is about to be married harbors dreams of life together. They envision a life filled with shared interests, common goals and values, mutual cares and concerns. Many newlyweds feel lucky on their wedding day—lucky to have met someone who understands them and shares their likes and dislikes, someone who is so obviously right for them! But no matter how ideally suited they are, at some point every husband and wife realize that theirs is not a perfect match. They realize that they do not always agree. They do not think, feel, and behave the same way. The merging of their two personalities, preferences, and backgrounds is much harder than they ever imagined.

Joseph F. Newton

❖ ❖

Young people imagine that once they are married they have laid in a stock of bliss that will last a lifetime. I would counsel them to gather daily fresh supplies of love. Let the same care and tenderness that has characterized the early days of lovemaking be your concern all the days of life, and you will find that marriage becomes an increasing blessing with the passing of the years.

❖ ❖

Remember that every marriage must be worked at for success. Every worthwhile thing in life must be worked for and marriage is no exception. Getting married is only the beginning; then comes the work, the deepening of love by the intelligent nurturing of that tender plant. Learning to listen, to share, to forgive. A happy marriage is the reward of effort and skill and discipline.

H. Richard Rasmusson

❖ ❖

One of the tragedies of our society is the increasing divorce rate and its long-term negative effects on children and families. Christians have tried to balance their strong support for the permanence of marriage and their tender care for those who live in the backwash of a marriage that dissolves.

❧ ❧

Divorce is clearly a breach of God's will for marriage. Divorce springs from a hardness of heart and the church needs to take a stand against the rising tide of easy divorce in our society. Many enter marriage today without any sense of it being a lifelong commitment. To have and to hold as long as we both shall live has been changed to as long as my spouse meets my needs and I am fulfilled. For Jesus, marriage is not a temporary, romantic alliance that can be terminated whenever one or both wish. On the other hand, the Church needs to communicate the grace of God and forgiveness of sin, including divorce. God hates divorce because, like all sin, it destroys. But God does not hate the divorced person. Therefore, the Church must balance on a tightrope by proclaiming God's forgiveness to sinners who violate that sanctity.

David E. Garland

❧ ❧

We live in a less than perfect world, and we are less than perfect people, and we often make a mess of our lives and our marriages. Divorce may be the only solution to an unredeemable

situation, but divorce is not the unpardonable sin. It is just another sign that we have not reached the ideal that God holds
for us.

John P. Dever

❖ REFLECTION ❖

As you read the following selection, consider your own
level of commitment to your spouse and your marriage.
Then think about one thing you can do this week to reaf-
firm your love and devotion to your mate.

84

❖ ❖

The Christian tradition emphasizes that marriage is based on a
commitment rather than a mere contract. That is to say, it accepts
from the very beginning the proposition that marriage is an unconditional relationship. It is for this reason that all traditional
wedding services call for pledges from both man and woman that
they will live together "from this day forward, for better, for
worse, for richer, for poorer, in sickness and in health, to love and
to cherish so long as we both shall live." This is both an idealis-
tic and a realistic approach to marriage. It is not to be a temporary affair. Hence the relationship is based not on a contract that
one negotiates but on a commitment pledged through an as-
tonishing act of faith.

M.K.W. Heicher

❖ ❖

❧ PRAYER ❧

Our heavenly Father, give to this man and this woman the ability to keep the vow and covenant made between them. Where selfishness would show itself, give love; where mistrust is a temptation, give confidence; where misunderstanding intrudes, give gentleness and patience.

C. Neil Strait

parenting

✤ ✤

Unless the Lord builds the house,
those who build it labor in vain.
Unless the Lord guards the city,
the guard keeps watch in vain.
It is vain that you rise up early
and go to bed late to rest,
eating the bread of anxious toil;
for he gives sleep to his beloved.

PSALM 127:1-2

He called a child, whom he put among them, and said,
"Truly I tell you, unless you change and become like
children, you will not enter the kingdom of heaven.
Whoever becomes humble like this child is the greatest
in the kingdom of heaven. Whoever welcomes one such
child in my name welcomes me."

MATTHEW 18:2-5

❧ ❧

One of the most challenging tasks we are called to do is to raise our children. The process is deceptively simple: guide them from the complete dependence of an infant to the complete independence of a mature adult. But every parent soon learns that it is not a simple process at all. Parenting requires courage, patience, persistence, and skill—and most of us are totally unprepared for the job! The following selections are not designed to give quick answers to all your parenting questions. Instead, you will find wisdom to guide you and encouragement to help you along the parenting path.

❧ ❧

In seeking to be responsible parents, we need to appreciate the power of our influence. Many people will affect the lives of our children—some in a positive way, others negatively. But no other people will so touch their lives as will mother and father.

Lee McGlone

❧ ❧

The first duty of parents is to care for their children with an unchanging love, a love that can never be gained by merit nor lost by failure. In life outside the home—in his school, among his friends, in the losses or gains of his adventures—a child doesn't always know where he stands. But within the home, a child should know where he stands—on the sure foundation of an unchanging love.

Harold E. Nicely

❧ ❧

How can I be a better parent? Let me suggest four simple things. First, you can share yourself with your children. This is what they want most. Then you can let them know that you love them. One thing that comforts me is that regardless of the mistakes we make, if our children know we care for them, they can endure almost any mistake. In the third place, you can enjoy them. Someone has said, "One way to be a bad parent is not to get any fun out of it." Finally, you can practice your own faith. When the ancient Jew said, "Train up a child in the way he should go, and when he is old he will not depart from it," he was speaking from both an act of faith and a deep conviction.

Luther Joe Thompson

89

❧ ❧

I remember when I laughed with my children—at the humorous plays they put on for the family, at the funny stories shared from school, when I fell for their tricks and catch questions. I recall the squeals of delight when I laughed with them and shared in their stunts on the lawn or living room floor. And I remember the times they told of these experiences with joyful expressions years later. I know that when I laughed with the children, our love was enlarged and the door was opened for doing many other things together.

John Drescher

❧ ❧

❧ REFLECTION ❧

Recall some of the closest times with your child or grand-child. Let the feelings of love and joy fill you again. What can you do today to express your affection and appreciation for your children, even if they are adults?

❧ ❧

It was hard for the disciples to imagine that Jesus could be in-terested in the welfare of little children during the busy days of his ministry. They tried to keep parents from bringing their chil-dren to Jesus. They did not want him to be bothered. What a shock it must have been for them to discover that these little children were the very ones for whom Jesus cared.

Clayton K. Harrop

❧ ❧

Reverence, respect, and love for the family require the decision to value the family over everything else in the world, including your individual personhood. A family is dedicated to the pri-macy of a family point of view. If your family does not come first—if the needs of any individual family member come be-fore the needs of the whole family—your family will not last!

Gary C. Redding

❧ ❧

90

If there is anything children can discern it is a fake. You can fool all of the people some of the time and you can fool some of the people all of the time, but you can't fool your children for long. That is why the foundation for a happy home is parents who are genuine.

Brian L. Harbour

❧ ❧

Christian parents have a deeper concern for their children than simply getting them to school on time and taking them on great family trips. We are also committed to their spiritual nurture and development. We bring our children to church for instruction and moral direction, but they learn far more from the spiritual life we model at home than they do in church.

91

❧ ❧

To neglect the spiritual training of children is to fail in the chief purpose of parenthood.

❧ ❧

Monica prayed faithfully for her son. When he was converted, this son, later known as Saint Augustine, said, "If I am thy child, O God, it is because thou didst give me such a mother."

❧ ❧

According to Deuteronomy 6, there are three things we must teach our sons and daughters: the first is that we teach about God, the second that we teach about grace, and the third that we teach guts. The most important thing, as mothers, fathers, grandparents, aunts, uncles, and neighbors, we ever teach our children is that *God is,* and that God is to be worshiped, enjoyed, and served forever. The very fabric of the universe is a gift. God has given us health, opportunity, and salvation in and through Jesus Christ. What we are called to do is respond, for the only response to grace is gratitude. Then finally there is a need to teach guts. If we fear the Lord, we will fear no one else.

Gary D. Stratman

92

❖ ❖

I know how Christian parents worry about pushing their children to make a profession of faith! But the solution is not to do nothing at all. Christian parents, listen! We pound into our kids' heads the necessity of making good grades and the urgency of getting a good college education. We repeatedly talk to our kids about responsible social and sexual behavior. We prod them toward success in everything they do. We spare no expense to make them pretty, poised, popular, positive, and prepared to face the world—and apparently we do it all with little or no reference to the Christian faith. Tell me, parents: What have you done to prepare your children to face God and eternity?

James W. Cox

❖ ❖

❧ PRAYER ❧

Father, you know what it is like to have a child who brings delight and joy. We, as parents, look at our children with the same sense of affection and pleasure. Thank you for these gifts of love to us. We also worry, Father, about their safety and grieve over their times of rebellion and wonder how we will ever make it through their growing up years. Help us to remember that our children are simply entrusted to us. In reality, they belong to you. Amen.

Douglas Connelly

"ONE BODY"

fellowship
and unity
in church life

❧ ❧

Christ loved the church and gave himself up for her.

EPHESIANS 5:25

For just as the body is one and has many members, and
all the members of the body, though many, are one
body, so it is with Christ. For in the one Spirit we were
all baptized into one body—Jews or Greeks, slaves or
free—and we were all made to drink of one Spirit.

1 CORINTHIANS 12:12-13

❖ ❖

*Christians are nurtured spiritually and emotionally in the context
of a Christian community called a church. We link our lives with
other Christians who can encourage us, help us, love us, and even
rebuke us. The New Testament uses several images to portray the
Church: a building, a hospital, a bride. The most striking image is
that we are a body and all of us are members of that body. No Christian can effectively function alone. As difficult as it sometimes is to
link our lives to a community of Christians, God has placed gifts
and resources in that community that you and I won't find anywhere else. We need each other. As you read through the selections in*

this chapter, think about your own church family and how you can deepen your commitment to your brothers and sisters in Christ.

❧ ❧

Believers, from the beginning, formed a community. It was within that community that each one found strength to carry on as an active Christian. To worship together, to study together, to begin to share together our joys and sorrows, our convictions, and our doubts—these are the marks of a living church of Christ, where we help one another to go on believing.

David H. C. Read

❧ ❧

The Church was meant to be a redemptive agency, a place where men and women would be confronted with God's Word in judgment and in love, a place where Christ is lifted up as Savior and Lord, a fellowship in which those who accept Christ can develop that relationship and, in turn, be forgiven, cleansed, and empowered by God's Spirit, and go out to influence others to follow Christ.

Odie M. Hoover Jr.

❧ ❧

The most significant happening in any community during the week is the Church's act of the public worship of God. It is this meeting with God that gives us the opportunity to see ourselves and our day and our deeds in the light of Christ's presence and God's purpose. Here we find forgiveness, renewal of life, and assurance. This fellowship of the Church is our barrier against despair and our emancipator from fear. Here in this Christian community of the Church, aspiration is renewed, hope is sustained, desire is kindled, wrong is forgiven, cowardice is shamed, sorrow is shared, life is empowered, and we come most surely into the presence of him who said, "I am the way, the truth, the life." And the Church is his Body.

Frederick M. Meek

❖ ❖

Because the Church is made up of imperfect people, no congregation is perfect. People with different personalities and varying perspectives come together with one goal: to bring glory to God. Building a sense of community is not easy, but when the world around us sees that spirit of unity, they will know we are truly Christ's followers.

❖ ❖

It is sometimes claimed that Jesus never gave us a definition of a Christian. Yet he has given us this simple test that is quite sufficient: "By this shall all men know that you are my disciples, if you have love for one another."

George Walter Fiske

❖ ❖

I would not limit God by saying that one must be a member of the Church to be a Christian. God works outside the Church. Yet if one understands that the Church is an institution committed to belief in God's grace and forgiveness, that it is entrusted with the work and mission of Jesus Christ, and that all who believe are of the same family, then every Christian should want to be a responsible member of God's Church. Those believers who have a case against the Church should stay with it to make the Church what it should be. Dropping out is copping out.

Bert Van Shoest

❖ ❖

You cannot find God in your spare moments.

Gardiner M. Day

❖ ❖

The servant's place is to be beside his master. This means faithfulness when times get tough. It means loyalty when others turn back. If the church is failing, the preacher disappointing, the choir out of tune, and the program unchallenging, we need to discipline ourselves to continue following, because Jesus is still there. It may not be much of a church, but if the Lord is there, I should be there, too!

Craig Skinner

❖ ❖

Discouraging as the Church's mission may be, we know that God is in it with us. He keeps us going, he guarantees that in the long run it will all be worthwhile, and he promises an unseen but eternal fruition of our labors. Because we are human, we should like to succeed, but we are not called to succeed. We are called to be faithful and obedient and to leave to God the issue of our service.

A. Leonard Griffith

❧ ❧

The one contact with the community of Christians that most of us have is weekly worship together. Some people think the church service is for their benefit or entertainment. In reality, we come for God's sake, and to seek ways to encourage other Christians.

99

❧ ❧

There is a sense in which if you come to church primarily to get something, you will go away empty; only when you come to give something, do something, will you get the real thing. If you come here to get a lift to carry you through the week, you may get it, but you will only get a lift when you come here to let yourself be humble in the presence of the mighty God of the universe and let his demands upon you be made known, no matter how hard they may be.

Theodore Parker Ferris

❧ ❧

The average person's idea of a good sermon is one that goes over his head and hits one of his neighbors.

Ross C. Crighton

⌁ ⌁

Jesus says, "I will build my Church," but although he is the master builder, he is not the only builder. Jesus never says, "I will build the Church myself"; rather, we are called to be "laborers together with God" in the work of building his Church. It is to be his work and our work together. It may well be that we cannot all work for Christ in the same way, but we can all work for him in some way.

Wilfred J. T. Brown

100

⌁ REFLECTION ⌁

What would church be like if we went there to give, to see new ways to demonstrate our commitment to Christ, to open ourselves in love to those around us?

⌁ ⌁

A church begins as a small, zealous flock seeking to win others, anxious to tell the community about Jesus Christ, so filled with love for their friends and driven by the love of Christ that is within them that the little church grows in numbers. Then a strange transformation takes place. Little by little it becomes an established organization, and the first thing you know, they have a tremendous building to care for. The work goes well and they are "self-supporting," but the old zeal is gone. Advertising techniques and other means replace personal witness and invitation. The organization is so busy that it takes all of their energies just to keep the machine moving, whether or not it is producing anything.

Paul P. Fryhling

❖ ❖

The congregation that is oriented toward today and tomorrow has a future. The congregation that is oriented toward yesterday may have a glorious past, but it probably does not have a future.

Lyle E. Schaller

101

❖ PRAYER ❖

We admit, Lord Jesus, that our church is not what it should be, mainly because those of us who make up the church are not what we should be. As we meet this week for worship, give us a new perception of why we are gathered and who we are gathered to please. Remind us that we are there to give, not just to get. Fill our church community, large or small, with such a spirit of love that those looking on will be convinced that we are truly your followers. Amen.

Douglas Connelly

"UNITED WITH HIM"

Baptism and the Lord's Supper

❧ ❧

Jesus came and said to them, "All authority in heaven and on earth has been given to me. Go therefore and make disciples of all nations, baptizing them in the name of the Father and of the Son and of the Holy Spirit, and teaching them to obey everything that I have commanded you. And remember, I am with you always, to the end of the age."

MATTHEW 28:18-20

For I received from the Lord what I also handed on to you, that the Lord Jesus on the night when he was betrayed took a loaf of bread, and when he had given thanks, he broke it and said, "This is my body that is for you. Do this in remembrance of me." In the same way he took the cup also, after supper, saying, "This cup is the new covenant in my blood. Do this, as often as you drink it, in remembrance of me." For as often as you eat this bread and drink the cup, you proclaim the Lord's death until he comes.

1 CORINTHIANS 11:23-26

❖ ❖

Christians meet together for worship and mutual encouragement. We also meet to observe simple rituals that remind us of the fundamental facts of our faith. Baptism and the Lord's Supper are sermons without words; we act out the message. These observances are often called sacraments, from a Latin word used to refer to the oath of allegiance taken by Roman soldiers in loyalty to the emperor. When we participate in a baptism service or a communion service, we are renewing our oath of allegiance to our "emperor," Jesus Christ.

Baptism takes many forms within the Christian community. Some Christians practice sprinkling; others immerse totally in water. Some Christians baptize infants in anticipation of faith; others baptize only those who have come to faith. Whatever form is used, Christians all agree that baptism pictures outwardly the spiritual reality that takes place inside a person. We have been washed clean by God's forgiveness. We have died to the old life and been raised up to a new life of commitment to Jesus.

❧ ❧

Faith and believing are the content of the Christian life; baptism is a form. Faith is the essence; baptism is a symbol. As a symbol, baptism does not save. The physical water of baptism does not wash away one's sins, regardless of the quantity of water or the mode by which it is administered; it has no power to cleanse. Our sins are not where they can be touched by water, and if they were, water would be powerless to affect them. Baptism is a sign on the outside of what has happened and is happening on the inside, the experience of the death and resurrection of Christ and the receiving of the Holy Spirit through the response of faith.

Frank H. Epp

❧ ❧

Baptism is a custom as old as the Christian enterprise. On the day of Pentecost, Peter answered those who asked, "What must we do to be saved?" with, "Repent and be baptized, every one of you, in the name of Jesus Christ." From then until now, the overwhelming practice of the Church has been to initiate new members with baptism.

John W. Meister

❧ ❧

The second practice of the church has several names: Communion, the Lord's Supper, the Lord's Table, the Eucharist (from a Greek word meaning "to give thanks"). As often as we receive the bread and wine (or grape juice), we are drawn back to Jesus' sacrifice of himself on the cross.

❧ ❧

The Lord's Supper is primarily a memorial of Christ. He said, "Do this in remembrance of me." The bread represents his broken body; the wine his blood shed for us. They remind us in a touching and powerful way of what he suffered for us, and so tend to renew our love and devotion to him. Our eating and drinking of them is a very striking symbol of our taking him as our Sacrificial Savior, of his entrance into our souls, and of our living spiritual union with him and all believers.

❧ ❧

Remember that Jesus Christ himself is the host of this table. The Lord's table is not your table or my table. It is not one particular church's table. It is the Lord's table. He is the one who took bread and broke it. He is the one who took the cup and shared it with his disciples. We come to this table at his invitation. He extends his hands to all Christians, to all sinners who will trust him, to come and commune with him at this table.

William Powell Tuck

❧ REFLECTION ❧

What do you think about more as you take Communion—your own failures or God's gracious forgiveness? Carve out some time before your next participation in Communion to reflect on Jesus' love for you.

❧ ❧

The Lord's Supper summons us to look away from the dreary frustrations of wrecked vows and broken dreams and toward a love that has borne our own sins on the cross.

❧ ❧

Of all the things in the Lord's Supper, this ought to come home to us with tremendous force: God thought we were worth dying for. And it is a very humbling thing and a staggering thing that, knowing ourselves for what we are, God should think we are worth so much.

❧ ❧

Communion, however, is more than a religious exercise. We are to be actively engaged in examining our lives before God. Whatever is not pleasing to him, we are to give over willingly to his forgiveness. We come to the Lord's table in need; we come away changed.

107

❧ ❧

What we celebrate at the Lord's table is not our worthiness but the worthiness of Jesus Christ. He welcomes all who come constrained by love and seeking to make their lives more worthy of him. Is there any danger that you and I are not worthy to partake of the Lord's Supper? Often people refuse to participate because they think they are not good enough. We come because we are not good enough and want to be better. If you have sinned, ask for forgiveness. If you are perplexed, seek God's guidance. If you are in sorrow, accept God's peace and comfort. Only if you have no appreciation of God's love, no reverence for the meaning of the Lord's Supper, and no intention of pleasing God do you have no right to come.

Myron J. Taylor

❧ ❧

The purpose of the Communion meal celebration is to be a reminder to us, to bring us back to the center of our faith, to be a stopping place for us to examine our lives, to see where we are going. It is a place for us to ask, What kind of bread have I been working for? Do I spend my days and my weeks working only for the bread that money can buy? Am I trying to satisfy my appetite with the tangible bread of things that rust, break apart, need paint, and burn oil? Is my life centered in the bread of what others think of me? Is it centered in the bread of power? Chasing the bread provided for us in the world is the rat race of life, getting us nowhere. When we consume Christ, absorbed in his teachings, his ways, his character, his mind, he becomes a part of us. He is the bread of life, and the life he gives is not characterized by chaos and frustration. The life he offers is eternal.

Craig A. Loscalzo

❧ PRAYER ❧

Lord Jesus, as our teeth crush the bread of Communion, remind us how you were crushed under the weight of our sin. As the tang of the wine floods our mouths, remind us of the bitter pain you bore as you poured out your life's blood for us. Most of all, remind us of the depth of your love for each one of us. Help us never to take your sacrifice for granted. Amen.

Douglas Connelly

108

"THE LORD IS MY SHEPHERD"

GUIDANCE

❧ ❧

Thus says the Lord,
your Redeemer, the Holy One of Israel:
"I am the Lord your God,
who teaches you for your own good,
who leads you in the way you should go."

ISAIAH 48:17

As for God, his way is perfect.

2 SAMUEL 22:31

If any of you is lacking in wisdom, ask God, who gives
to all generously and ungrudgingly, and it will be
given you.

JAMES 1:5

❧ ❧

*I don't know of any single issue that Christians struggle with more
than guidance: Which direction in life should I go? Who should I
marry? What career should I pursue? What decision should I make?
We want God to tell us what is best or which choice will bring happiness and security. But when we ask God for an answer, usually he
is silent. What we discover when we come to the Bible is that God*

promises to give us wisdom, not answers. We want voice-from-heaven direction; God offers quiet, unspectacular one-step-at-a-time wisdom.

❧ ❧

We cannot always trace God's hand, but we can always trust his heart.

Vance Havner

❧ ❧

112   God guides us, despite our uncertainties and our vagueness, even through our failings and mistakes. Only afterward, as we look back over the way we have come and reconsider certain important moments in our lives in the light of all that has followed them, or when we survey the whole progress of our lives, do we experience the feeling of having been led without knowing it, the feeling that God has mysteriously guided us.

Paul Tournier

❧ ❧

You aren't likely to be sent out under the will of God to do startling, impossible things. You are likely to be sent out to do the quiet, unspectacular things that matter, precisely where you are and with what you have.

Paul E. Scherer

❧ ❧

When God shuts a door, he opens a window.

John Ruskin

❖ ❖

In the Bible, when God wanted to give direct guidance to someone, he had no problem communicating clearly. God spoke from a burning bush, in a voice of thunder, or through a prophet's words. God can still speak that way today if he wants to. Most of the time, however, God speaks in quieter, more indirect ways—through the gentle whisper of his Spirit, through open and closed doors of opportunity, through the wisdom of a mature friend.

113

❖ ❖

Sometimes God uses our minds to bring us thoughts that we would not otherwise think, thoughts that intuitively tell us whether it would be foolish to go on or stay behind. Sometimes he uses our emotions, and when we are in tune with him, we can accept those emotions as guidance from him. All these thoughts and all these different feelings should be listened to as, other things being equal, they are the very voice of God trying to get through to us.

Glenn Clark

❖ ❖

Be serious about making decisions. Bathe the decision-making process in prayer and reexamine it all under the searching light of Scripture. Yield all anxieties and fears about planning to God. Go ahead and make the decision. Then act on the decision with timeliness, trusting God to oversee the results. Jesus made his decisions this way. His method will surely work for us as well.

James Earl Massey

❧ ❧

Life comes to us one day at a time. We may waste mental energy regretting yesterday and while away time presuming upon tomorrow. Yet life comes to us simply day by day. We should not let concern for tomorrow overwhelm us today. You could grow so worried about what the future will bring that you cannot face the present. No amount of anxiety will bring tomorrow sooner, and no thought contains the power to change what will occur when it gets here.

James L. Heflin

❧ ❧

God is not limited in his plans for us. Even our mistakes and failures don't trip him up. God can take the worst of our decisions and ultimately bring good from them.

❧ ❧

Life is a journey. It is a series of changes and transitions. There is no utopia, no stationary place, because life is a process. The journey metaphor makes room for failure. Journeys are seldom made without incident, without occurrences that redirect our lives: detours, dead-end streets, accidents, weariness, traffic jams, getting lost. Journeys include these interruptions, and so does life.

Ben Campbell Johnson

❖ ❖

We never face a situation in life devoid of God's presence. He is always opening up fresh possibilities in the face of every difficulty. With him there is always a way out.

Colbert S. Cartwright

115

❖ REFLECTION ❖

How can you let God guide a decision you are trying to make? Ask him for wisdom and his presence in your deliberations, and then believe that you will receive what you ask for!

❖ ❖

If we find ourselves in a situation in which God seems to be silent, in which there seems to be no word from God, we will do well to act on the last word from God that we heard.

Carlyle Marney

❖ ❖

The greatest discovery I made in life was that God was probably right when I thought him to be wrong.

Reuben A. Torrey

❧ ❧

The detours of life are often begun by a dead end. We literally back out and start all over again. The death of one direction is the birth of a new one. Old things must pass away in order that all things be made new. Much of our kicking, screaming, complaining, depression, and projection of blame onto others is little more than our steadfast refusal to get on with life, and our desire to hang on to a patently dead past.

Wayne E. Oates

116

❧ PRAYER ❧

Comforting Lord, we come to you as sheep, needing direction, exhausted from trying to find our way through life without you. In our darkness, we pray for light; in our indecision, we pray for wisdom; in our obsession to see the next step on the path, we pray for the patience to wait for you. Amen.

Douglas Connelly

"RICH GENEROSITY"

Money

❧ ❧

God is able to give you more than you need, so that you will always have all you need for yourselves and more than enough for every good cause.

2 CORINTHIANS 9:8, NEW ENGLISH BIBLE

Blessed are you, O Lord, the God of our ancestor Israel, forever and ever. Yours, O Lord, are the greatness, the power, the glory, the victory, and the majesty; for all that is in the heavens and on the earth is yours; yours is the kingdom, O Lord, and you are exalted as head above all. Riches and honor come from you, and you rule over all. In your hand are power and might; and it is in your hand to make great and to give strength to all. And now, our God, we give thanks to you and praise your glorious name.

KING DAVID IN 1 CHRONICLES 29:10-13

❖ ❖

Most of us think we give God his share of our money when we drop a check in the offering plate on Sunday morning. The Bible challenges that perspective by declaring that God owns everything. "The earth is the Lord's and the fullness thereof" (Psalm 24:1). Every-thing we own and earn belongs to God! We have simply been en-trusted with its use. God is just as concerned about the money we keep for ourselves as he is about the money we give away. Our check-books and credit card statements more accurately reflect our prior-ities than the money we put in the offering plate.

⤙ ⤚

Though we cannot serve God *and* money, we can serve God *with* money.

Ernest Thompson

120

⤙ ⤚

Money is the most overrated commodity on today's market of values. It can buy a house, but it cannot make a home. It can pay for medicine, but it cannot purchase health. It can acquire things, but things do not satisfy the soul.

James McGraw

⤙ ⤚

When you look at the life of Jesus, in addition to the purity of his speech and the purity of his thought-life, one of the things you are immediately aware of is the purity of his attitude to-ward material things. Jesus possessed his possessions; his pos-sessions did not possess him. Someone suggested that there are two ways to be rich. One is in the abundance of your possessions. The other is in the fewness of your wants. When we depend on Christ to supply us with our daily needs, our wants become few indeed. We become children again—simple, happy, and unafraid.

Arthur McPhee

❖ ❖

"Do not store up for yourselves treasures on earth, where moth and rust consume and where thieves break in and steal; but store up for yourselves treasures in heaven, where neither moth nor rust consumes and where thieves do not break in and steal. For where your treasure is, there your heart will be also."

Jesus in Matthew 6:19–21

Temporary holdings do not constitute real riches. God wants us to possess. He wants us to have, but he wants us to have the best. Jesus says, "If you keep your fortune on earth, you have made a fortune and stored it in a place where you cannot hold it. Make your fortune, but store it in a place where you can keep it. Invest it in the Kingdom of God and let it draw interest compounded throughout eternity. For where your treasure is, there will your heart and interest and attention be focused also."

Frank Pollard

❖ ❖

If all your treasure is in the things of this world, you don't have anything! But if you have Jesus in your heart, there is no person on the face of the Earth who is richer than you are!

Randy Smith

❖ ❖

May our earning and our spending, our saving and our giving, whatever we do with the wealth of our hands, be done in the name of our Lord Jesus Christ, and may it express unto thee, O God, the thanksgiving in our hearts for the blessings of Christ. Amen.

122

M.K.W. Heicher

❖ ❖

God does not use arm-twisting to motivate us to give to those around us who are in need and to the work of God's Kingdom. We are motivated to give by gratitude. If God could so abundantly bless us in Christ and then give us so much material wealth besides, how can we respond to him with anything less than willing generosity and sacrifice?

❖ ❖

For God, the gift that counts is the gift that costs. True giving
has to be measured according to what is left, not only according to what is given. It is not so much the size of the gift but
the sacrifice involved in the gift.

Harold Freeman

❧ ❧

Great faith produces generous giving.

Ernest White

❧ ❧

123

The Christian lifestyle is one of self-denial. It is the life that responds to the call to say no to yourself and your personal desires
and needs. It is the life dedicated to voluntarily doing without,
to voluntarily going without, to voluntarily depending on God
for your total welfare and well-being.

Gary C. Redding

❧ REFLECTION ❧

How does the perspective of God's ownership and God's
abundance change your view of giving? What one possession could you give away that you know someone else
would cherish?

❧ ❧

The wonderful thing about the purse is that it can help you be a better Christian. It can extend all your powers. The money can travel for you all around the world and do good. It can go where you do not have time to go personally. It can serve people you will never even be able to meet. It can serve a variety of causes although you could not possibly have time, strength, or energy to deal personally with all of them. Your money will do so much for you. It will extend your enthusiasm. It will extend what you know and how you feel and your passion to serve. It will become an instrument of God's holy purpose if you give it a chance, by dedicating it to Christ!

Lowell H. Atkinson

124

❧ ❧

Jesus cared about the poor and constantly emphasized his concern for them, but Jesus did not worry half so much about the moral estate of the poor as he did about the moral estate of the rich. He feared the possession of money as a major peril. We are all concerned about that portion of the population that lacks money enough for a decent livelihood. Were Jesus here, he would also be concerned about the moral estate of those of us who have enough.

Harry Emerson Fosdick

❧ ❧

❧ PRAYER ❧

Help us, O Lord, to use well the wealth that comes into our hands. May we see clearly the opportunities to give and do good, and thus to bring joy to ourselves and others.

M.K.W. Heicher

"DELIVER US FROM THE EVIL ONE"

Temptation

❖ ❖

Do not enter the path of the wicked,
and do not walk in the way of evildoers.
Avoid it; do not go on it;
turn away from it and pass on.

PROVERBS 4:14-15

No testing has overtaken you that is not common
to everyone. God is faithful, and he will not let you
be tested beyond your strength, but with the testing
he will also provide the way out so that you may be
able to endure.

1 CORINTHIANS 10:13

❖ ❖

*The plaque over my friend's computer says it all: Opportunity only
knocks once; temptation leans on the doorbell. Temptation brings
different things to mind for each one of us. For some, it's a hot fudge
sundae even though we are overweight and are fighting high blood
pressure. For a businessperson or parent under unrelenting pressure,
temptation may be another drink or two beyond the point of control. Maybe temptation has to do with the local video store or adult
Internet sites.*

You know what it is in your life that draws you away from God's desire and will—and I know what it is in my life. The question is, How can we overcome and resist the lure of that temptation? It certainly starts by recognizing that God's power is available to help us. God's promise is that we won't be tempted beyond our capacity to turn away. But just as important, we need to be prepared to resist before *the temptation arrives.*

❧ ❧

Always put off until tomorrow what you shouldn't do at all.

❧ ❧

Temptation in the Bible has two chief meanings. The first is that "inward prompting" or desire to sin. This is the element that does battle with our consciences. The devil uses temptations to hurt us and bring us down. The second main sense means trials or testing and refers to circumstances in life that test a person's faith and courage. These sanctify life and build character. God tests people; he does it to help us grow. God is interested in our best; the devil is interested in our demise.

Jeffrey T. Timm

❧ ❧

Life is short and time is precious. We simply do not have time to waste our minds and energies on things that tear us down. We ought to measure everything we read, everything we see, everything we do by this standard: Does it build me up in body, mind, and spirit? Does it make my life purer and nobler? Or does it tear down and degrade my life? Christians do not have the right to watch or indulge in anything that does not build them up and make them stronger and better-informed servants of God.

Wayne E. Ward

❖ REFLECTION ❖

One source of help for dealing with temptation is to develop an accountability relationship with a Christian friend. Think about a person you can talk with honestly, someone you know will pray for you and love you. As you consider asking that friend about becoming accountable to each other, what fears or questions come to mind? Ask God to give you direction.

129

❖ ❖

When you run from temptation, don't leave a forwarding address.

Allan Wooters

❖ ❖

If I am a Christian, why am I tempted? I have had a conversion experience, I am supposed to be a changed person, I am trying to follow the teachings of Jesus the best I know how—so why am I sometimes tempted?

No one who has ever walked the earth has been exempt from temptation. It's a part of being human. The key is never to think that we are above temptation. Nor should we think that because we have been tempted we have sinned. Our task is to be prepared to deal with temptation when it does come.

Four simple steps might be of help to us:

1. *Know and name your temptation.* Identify what is tempting you—money, lust, adultery, illegal drugs, anger, violence, dishonesty, cheating on an exam, overeating. It's easier to deal with your enemy when he is out in the open.

2. *Design a plan of resistance.* Take precautions to stay away from whatever is tempting you or from situations that could prove to be unhealthy.

3. *Look to the example of Jesus.* The writer of the book of Hebrews says, "Because he himself was tested by what he suffered, he is able to help those who are being tested" (2:18). Jesus relied on prayer, Scripture, and the power of the Spirit to help him be victorious over his temptations. So can we.

4. *Call for help from God and others.* Spend time in prayer with God in which you name the temptation before God and ask for spiritual help. We can count on God's help to strengthen us. "God is faithful," the Scripture says, and he will provide us a way out of our temptation and testing (1 Corinthians 10:13). And talk to a friend, pastor, or counselor so that you will have some emotional and spiritual support.

Randy Hammer

One continuing source of strength when we face temptation is the knowledge that Jesus knows how it feels to be under attack. He can sympathize with us, and give us the courage to turn away.

❧ ❧

The Son of God faced the full force of the devil's attack. How wonderful that the Lord we worship has "been through it," suffering every kind of temptation. He is not distant and remote but a Lord who can sympathize and understand, a Lord who can help, a Lord who shows us how to face temptation and conquer in his strength.

Michael Baughen　　131

❧ **PRAYER** ❧

Lead us away from the temptation that caused us to fall yesterday. Help us to say no to the suggestion of evil before the substance of it appears. Let us not look in the direction of our old sins lest we walk toward them in our weakness. Guide our steps along the paths where we shall think of the things that are true and honest and pure and lovely and of good report. Keep us so close to you that evil may lose its lure. Take not your hand from the helm of our lives lest we drift into the storms where desire or passion may prove too great for our strength.

Ralph W. Sockman

"WHATEVER YOU DO"

work

❧ ❧

Do you see those who are skillful in their work?
they will serve kings;
they will not serve common people.

PROVERBS 22:29

Whatever your task, put yourselves into it, as done for
the Lord and not for your masters, since you know that
from the Lord you will receive the inheritance as your
reward; you serve the Lord Christ.

COLOSSIANS 3:23-24

❖ ❖

Whether we work in the home or outside the home, whether we are
employees or employers or self-employed, we all have work to do.
The Bible says that you can tell a lot about a person by watching
how that person works. The Bible also makes it clear that all of life
is important to God. Our time at work is just as much God's con-
cern as our time in church. In fact, how you and I act on the job
reveals more about our commitment to Christ than how we act
on Sunday.

❖ ❖

Almost without exception we can serve and glorify God more fully and effectively where we work than anywhere else.

Robert J. McCracken

❧ ❧

On Sundays we talk about a world of grace, where everything is given to us, where we are loved unconditionally just for who we are, where life is more about being than doing, where the highest values are love and community. It is a world of abundance. Then on Mondays most of us enter a world where, to put it mildly, we are saved not by grace but by our own works, where the ultimate question is our productivity, where our worth is measured by what we have accomplished and how efficient and effective we are, where the deepest values are ambition, competition, and success. It is often a world of scarcity, in which only the strongest survive; it worships at the altar of profits. Yet Christians have always believed that the Lord of the universe is also the Lord of the marketplace and that there should be no wall between our faith and our work. We can't simply live separate, parallel lives. What we do on Sunday is intended to shape and inform what we do all week long at work, and what we do at work should be the expression of our souls, the acting out of the convictions we express on Sunday morning.

Samuel T. Lloyd III

134

❧ ❧

So we don't work just to make money and pay bills and put our children through college. We also work to express our devotion to our "real" boss, Jesus Christ.

~ ~

One of the most attractive elements of the Christian faith is that it turns the workplace into a place of worship. The Bible says that Jesus is so interested in me that he wants me to think of all the work I do as something I do for him. People who believe in Jesus Christ and who are part of the workforce would have an unusual answer if someone were to ask them, "Why are you working?" They would say, "I am doing this because Jesus wants me to do it. I am doing it for him. I am doing it as well as I can because I don't want to present inferior work to Jesus. Christ has saved me, and he wants me to do everything, even my work, for his glory.

Joel Nederhood

135

~ **REFLECTION** ~

Envision what your workplace would be like if every person's goal was to work in such a way that Jesus would approve. What would change? How would your attitude and behavior change?

~ ~

There is a sense in which we witness by the way we do our job. A poor employee and a good witness never go together.

Kenneth Chafin

❧ ❧

Where do we get the idea that work is a curse? Not from God. "And the Lord God took the man and put him into the Garden of Eden to dress it and keep it." That was the work assignment before Adam and Eve rebelled. It was a great job. No problem but pure joy. Labor is not bad; it is a blessing. Not a curse but a comfort. In the Bible, work is always discussed in the most positive terms.

C. W. Bess

❧ ❧

Work is also designed to give us the resources we need to care for people in need. Giving to others is not an afterthought but part of our planning as we divide up our paycheck.

❧ ❧

Do good, honest work (Ephesians 5:28). Paul first tells those who might be thieves at heart, or in actual practice, to stop stealing and to put forth legitimate effort to increase their wealth and prosperity. It is a call to personal responsibility. To take Paul seriously, one must seriously apply one's physical skills and intelligence in plying a trade or pursuing a career that will, with honest labor, lead to satisfying one's own needs. But Paul takes this idea a step further. We are to work not just to squeak by but to have sufficient increase to have something to share with those who lack adequate resources. Paul is not calling for an institutional response to the needy but a personal one! Just as we are challenged to get our hands involved in making a living, we are also encouraged to get our hands and hearts involved in sharing the fruits of our labor with others.

Kenneth B. Stout

❖ ❖

Human beings are created to work. When the New Testament talks about the opposite of work, it does not talk about leisure; it talks about stealing. In 2 Thessalonians we read, "If any will not work, neither let him eat."

Joel Nederhood

❖ ❖

We are not only to pursue excellence in our work; we are also to have an urgency about our work. If everything we do is to please Christ and if our every effort contributes to God's Kingdom, then we are to be conscious of the limited time we have in this life to mark the lives of those around us.

❖ ❖

Today is all you have. We have heard, "There is no time like the present." That is incorrect. We should say, "There is no time *but* the present." The apostle Paul recognized the importance of making a mountain of the moment. To the Ephesians he wrote, "Making the most of your time, because the days are evil" (Ephesians 5:16). Making the most of your time means to redeem the time, to buy up every opportunity.

Max R. Hickerson

❧ PRAYER ❧

Almighty God, go with us into the work of this new week. Bestow on us strength for our burdens, wisdom for our responsibilities, insight to meet the demands of our time. May the things that command our interest enrich our souls.

Robert J. McCracken

"SEEK GOOD, NOT EVIL"

Justice

❧ ❧

But let justice roll down like waters,
and righteousness like an ever-flowing stream.

AMOS 5:24

What does the Lord require of you but to do justice,
and to love kindness, and to walk humbly with your
God?

MICAH 6:8

Religion that is pure and undefiled before God, the
Father, is this: to care for orphans and widows in their
distress, and to keep oneself unstained by the world.

JAMES 1:27

❖ ❖

*Cries for justice are all around us. They echo from overcrowded
prisons, violent inner cities, forgotten children, and oppressed mi-
norities. As Christians, our answer to these cries is to act differently from everyone else in our culture. God calls us to act justly.*

Although it is not widely known, activist Christians have been the ones who have initiated most of the courageous social reforms in our history. The development of schools, the building of hospitals, the movement to abolish slavery, the reform of prisons, and the struggle for civil rights all had their roots in the desire of Christians to pursue God's justice in an unjust world.

❧ ❧

The Church must be reminded that it is not the master of the state but rather the conscience of the state.

Martin Luther King Jr.

142

❧ ❧

Your Word, "Follow me!" O Lord, reaches into our lives and moves our hearts. How often we hear your call yet fail to heed it! We know the shining path but walk in darkness. Help us, O God, to seek your Kingdom in all those places where our lives are immersed—in our homes, offices, workshops, schools, communities. As citizens of the state, the nation, and the world, whether our duties be small or great, help us to work diligently for the rule of God in the affairs of human beings.

❧ ❧

William Lloyd Garrison, in the middle of the nineteenth century, goaded America's drowsy, sluggish conscience against the heinous crime of human slavery. "I will not be silent. I will not excuse. I will not equivocate. I will not retreat a single inch, and I will be heard."

Milton B. Eastwick

❖ ❖

Grant, O God, that your holy and life-giving Spirit may so move every human heart (and especially the hearts of the people of this land), that barriers which divide us may crumble, suspicions disappear, and hatreds cease; that our divisions be healed, we may live in justice and peace; through Jesus Christ our Lord.

The Book of Common Prayer

143

❖ REFLECTION ❖

What injustice that you see in the world around you bothers you most? Do you know of any organizations that directly address that social need? If not, find out who they are and ask God to help you discern some ways in which you can be personally involved in bringing God's justice into that arena.

❖ ❖

Love must be learned, and learned again and again; there is no end of it. Hate needs no instruction, but waits only to be provoked.

Katherine Anne Porter

❖ ❖

Good works are meant to glorify God, not our egos. They are intended to enrich our community, not our wallets. They are meant to share Christ, not to display our goodness for the purpose of public adulation.

Richard Andersen

❧ ❧

I suppose that until the Kingdom comes in our imperfect society, prisons will be necessary. What disturbs me most are not the walls of brick and iron but the walls that have so often led directly to prison walls and that confine many others in our society. These are the walls of poverty, with all its limiting circumstances; the walls of prejudice, whether racial, religious, or economic; the walls of substandard education and early dropouts; the walls of dismal and overcrowded housing and slum surroundings; the walls of oversized families with neither enough material goods nor loving attention to go around; the walls where alcohol and drunkenness do their disastrous work; the walls of tension and anger in both poor families and those that are wealthy; the walls of too great leniency without discipline. Such walls, found throughout the land, are more confining than any prison.

Georgia Harkness

❧ ❧

It isn't hard to see that the work of standing against injustice is not finished. Every new example of injustice challenges God's peo-

*ple to emerge from the padded pews of our comfortable churches
and labor in the dark places of oppression and wrong.*

❧ ❧

Love is constantly creative. It cannot be forever silent; it must
speak out. It cannot be forever idle; it must reach out. Something always comes of love. It changes a house into a home, a
relationship into a companionship, an interest into a concern,
an offering into a sacrifice, a responsibility into a mission. It
gives us strength in moments of weakness; it grants us courage
in times of fear.

Arnold H. Lowe 145

❧ **PRAYER** ❧

Let us learn how to care for the family of humanity, Father. May we be disturbed and uneasy as long as there are
homeless folks among us, hungry folks about us, lonely
folks everywhere. May we be disturbed and uneasy as long
as war is waged, as long as racism is rampant, as long as
hatred is harbored among us.

W. Henry Fields

in the

shadow

and in

the light

Life is a mysterious mixture of joy and sorrow, peace and unrest, prosperity and struggle. Over the course of our lives, we come to see that in every situation we learn new things about God. When we are discouraged, we learn to draw strength from God's presence and love. When we enjoy success or a promotion, our hearts overflow with gratitude for God's goodness. When we fail, we learn what it feels like to be forgiven and cleansed.

The next group of chapters explores the light and the shadows, experiences of joy and experiences of pain. Look for at least one chapter that speaks to your heart today, and be ready for another that will speak to you tomorrow or next week. You might have a friend or spouse who is walking in one of life's shadows right now. Share some of the wise counsel you discover in these pages. Be an instrument that God uses to bring blessing and hope.

Advancement and success

❖ ❖

May the Lord grant you your heart's desire,
and fulfill all your plans.
May we shout for joy over your victory,
and in the name of our God set up our banners.
May the Lord fulfill all your petitions.

PSALM 20:4-5

This one thing I do: forgetting what lies behind and
straining forward to what lies ahead, I press on toward
the goal for the prize of the heavenly call of God in
Christ Jesus.

PAUL IN PHILIPPIANS 3:13-14

❖ ❖

*Some Christians look at success with suspicion. They think that any-
one who has gained wealth or influence or fame has somehow com-
promised their loyalty to Christ. The men and women of the Bible,
however, never lived under that delusion. Wealth or fame acquired
by dishonest or disrespectful means was certainly not applauded, but
genuine success was seen as a gift from the Lord's hand. Abraham
and Job and Solomon were fabulously wealthy. David's name re-
sounded throughout the biblical world as a military and political
leader.*

Success, of course, is measured in many different ways. Some committed, faithful Christians have very little name recognition in society. Most of us are not wealthy or in positions of political power. But success is certainly not to be feared. If God gives you influence or wealth, embrace it—and then use it as a platform to further God's Kingdom.

❧ ❧

If a person could look into the future and see what God has planned for his life, he would jump for joy. The life God has planned for you is full of adventure, achievement, courage, and love.

Perry Tanksley

❧ ❧

Every Christian ought to be an optimist. He ought to expect great things because he believes in a great God. He is sure of the future because he is sure of God.

❧ ❧

Success: Getting up once more than you fall down.

❧ ❧

True success, of course, does not come easily. God doesn't simply drop success into our laps. He expects us to work diligently and honorably to achieve our goals and dreams.

❧ ❧

Races are not won merely by initial talent; they are won by discipline and incessant training. The athlete is quite unwilling to leave things to chance, to settle for things half done. In the Christian context, nothing is good enough for God except the best a person can do, no matter what it costs.

Harold Blake Walker

153

❧ ❧

God uses people who are prepared to do his work. One person is prepared by poverty to do the work of God, another by being born into wealth. One person can make himself available to God for work among some people by the very fact that he has not seen much of the schools; another is able to serve God most effectively among other people because he has had superior training. God uses people of different backgrounds to reach people of varied backgrounds. The important thing is what God will make of what is made available to him. The Bible tells us that God has taken the common and despised things of this earth and made them into vessels of honor for his service. The Lord uses prepared persons, but they are the ones who have humility before God to say, "Lord, here am I. Send me. Use me as you wish. Show me what I can do and enable me to do it. What I may do in my own strength, I do not do well; but what I do in your strength can be pleasing to you."

❖ ❖

Within the context of the Christian community, the measure of success changes. Jesus lived a life of sacrifice and faith. He said that the greatest person in his Kingdom was not the one with the most toys or the greatest name recognition, but the one most willing to serve.

❖ ❖

"If anyone would be first, he must be last of all and servant of all." Here is the central Word of Jesus' teaching about life in the Kingdom of God. It turns the thought processes of every generation upside down. The ordinary barometers of greatness are cast aside as obsolete. Pomp and circumstance, power, glory, and adulation are irrelevant. True greatness would now be measured by one's willingness to pour out his or her life for others—to be a servant of all.

Lee R. McGlone

❖ ❖

God has not called me to be successful; he has called me to be faithful.

Mother Teresa

❖ ❖

Jesus took the world's standard of greatness and stood it on its head. Many businesses are organized on the theory of a pyramid, and the higher you climb toward the apex, the nearer you get to the top, the more people you have under you, the more power you exert. Jesus flipped the pyramid upside down. Jesus' diagram of greatness is that the nearer you get to the apex, the more people you carry in love, the greater responsibility you have for others. It's just the opposite of the world's standard. You don't swagger into the kingdom—you bow, you surrender, you submit your will to the Father's.

Alton H. McEachern

❖ REFLECTION ❖

How successful do you consider yourself? Meditate on how successful you are in serving, in carrying other people in love.

❖ ❖

The ascent of Christ into heaven answers Christ's descent into humanity, humility, and crucifixion. The crown follows the cross. Triumph follows suffering. Reward follows service. Up follows down. The pattern characterizes Christ and it must characterize the Christian. The measure of the ascent is more than equal to the measure of the descent into suffering and service.

Roderick K. Durst

❖ ❖

We all need dreams. We need to have a vision of what we are supposed to be doing as human beings; that's why we accept Jesus Christ as our Lord. We want to become, in the grace of God, like Jesus.

Rick Brand

✤ PRAYER ✤

O God—Giver of Life, Provider, Author of Salvation, Determiner of Destiny—the image of ourselves diminishes to nothing as we come into your presence; and yet, Lord, we learn that we are valuable in your sight. Help us to accept our worth and prove it by the surrender of our lives to your will and by the committal of our powers to your purposes. In whatever circumstance or condition of life we find ourselves, may we take the opportunity to grow, to invest our talents in serving you, and to live lives worthy of the gospel of Jesus Christ; in his name we pray. Amen.

"IN YOUR ANGER DO NOT SIN"

anger

❧ ❧

One who is slow to anger is better than the mighty,
and one whose temper is controlled than one who
captures a city.

PROVERBS 16:32

Be angry but do not sin; do not let the sun go down
on your anger, and do not make room for the devil. . . .
Put away from you all bitterness and wrath and anger
and wrangling and slander, together with all malice,
and be kind to one another, tenderhearted, forgiving
one another, as God in Christ has forgiven you.

EPHESIANS 4:26-27, 31-32

❖ ❖

*Anger wipes out so many good things. It ruins churches and family
reunions and marriages. It has a way of disarming us and defeat-
ing us. Those of us who struggle with anger find ourselves lashing
out—usually at the wrong people, at the wrong time, and in the
wrong way. When that kind of anger is in control of our hearts and
words, God is not in control.*

*Human nature seems bent toward violence and anger, but the
Christian has someone who can help bring control. God's Spirit*

within us says, "That's far enough." When we listen to God, anger's powerful grip is loosened.

❦ ❦

You're never at your best when you are angry.

❦ ❦

To get angry is to be human. The issue for Jesus, however, is how we handle our anger. The New English Bible is correct in translating Matthew 5:22, "Everyone who *nurses* anger. . . ." Problems come when we feed anger and justify it so that it continues to grow like a cancer. Problems come when we deal with our anger inappropriately. Some people attempt to deny their anger. They go into withdrawal and try to pretend that nothing is wrong. They engage in cold warfare. It is difficult to deal with someone's anger when they refuse to talk. Others handle their anger through guerilla warfare. They use hit-and-run tactics, and the victim frequently has no idea who or what hit them. Others ventilate their anger. They are like nuclear warheads. They explode, and everyone around is wiped out by the fallout. Anger is like pain; it gives us a warning. We need to pay attention to it so that we can make changes in our lives to correct the problem. Jesus would have us use our anger creatively. We should deal with annoying differences honestly so they do not destroy our relationship with another. We need to go to our brother or sis-

160

ter quickly to resolve the problems before they become impossible to resolve.

David E. Garland

❖ ❖

We're going to quit being defeated by unworthy opponents. We're going to quit making a fuss over petty trials. You have a bad temper; quit making excuses—control it! Some people control more temper in five minutes than you have in five days.

M.K.W. Heicher

❖ ❖

The immediate temptation when someone does us wrong is to retaliate, to get revenge. But revenge only ends when one side says "Enough!" It takes real courage to say "Enough!" It takes making one of the most difficult decisions you will ever make: the decision to live with an uneven score.

Ronald Higdon

❖ REFLECTION ❖

Picture yourself when you are angry. Try to see how you appear to your children or friends. Now picture yourself in a joyful, patient mood. Which spirit permeates your life most often, and in which mood do you want others to remember you?

❖ ❖

Children sense the weakness of adults. Children are especially sensitive to the weakness betrayed in an uncontrollable temper. Angry adults sometimes think their loud voice and pounding fist speak to children of strength, power, and force. It doesn't take a child long, however, to learn that when father or mother are like that, they are, in fact, out of control.

Gary C. Redding

❖ ❖

The soft answer that turns away wrath also makes it easier if you have to eat your words.

162

Dorthea Kent

❖ ❖

Jesus often blazed with anger. When he was confronted with injustice or exploitation, he always responded with righteous anger toward those who were responsible. Men and women who put petty rules or personal greed above compassion for hurting people felt the full brunt of Jesus' sharp words. As our society has become more prone to rage, we have seen an alarming decline in "righteous anger" and an equally alarming rise in "unrighteous anger." We get angry when someone gets in our way or doesn't do what we want them to do. We are quick to defend our "rights," but the poor and oppressed aren't worth much of our time. We are no longer outraged at public wrong or glaring injustice.

❖ ❖

Anger is not always the opposite of love; sometimes it is love's clearest expression. Anger can give love courage. A weakness of our generation is the lack of righteous indignation in the face of present evils. Perhaps our greatest tragedy is not the strident clamor of bad people but the appalling silence of good people. Too few are angry enough to speak out.

Luther Joe Thompson

❧ ❧

God has given us the capacity for anger as part of our equipment. Rightly used and for a good cause, anger releases power.

David A. MacLennan

❧ ❧

Express sinless anger (Ephesians 5:26). This seems to be a strange piece of advice. For one thing, we tend to think of anger as inherently wrong. Why should Paul be advising these new believers to show any kind of anger at all? Perhaps Paul is recognizing what we sometimes call "righteous indignation"—a healthy, even wholesome, anger that is a response to some terrible injustice and that is not based on selfishness or pride.

Kenneth B. Stout

❧ ❧

God loves us the way we are, but he loves us too much to leave us that way.

Leighton Ford

❧ ❧

❧ PRAYER ❧

Spirit of God, we need your control. We can be very pleasant and patient at church, but within the walls of our homes or behind the steering wheels of our vehicles, anger is a real problem. Remove the tangled web of bitterness and frustration that casts a negative shroud over our hearts. Show us the deeply rooted feelings of revenge or jealousy that need to be pulled out and discarded. Come into the temples of our hearts and sweep them clean. Amen.

Douglas Connelly

"I WILL TAKE HOLD OF YOUR HAND"

comfort

❧ ❧

Those who wait for the Lord
shall renew their strength,
they shall mount up with wings like eagles,
they shall run and not be weary,
they shall walk and not faint.

ISAIAH 40:31

"My grace is sufficient for you, for power is made
perfect in weakness."

JESUS TO PAUL IN 2 CORINTHIANS 12:9

❖ ❖

*In the worst experiences of life, we don't need heavy theology or a
series of self-help exercises. We need to know that someone cares.
Family and friends can bring wonderful help to us. Counselors
and pastors can provide assurance and hope. But when we're all
alone, when we stare at the ceiling late at night through tear-filled
eyes, comfort can come only from God. We sense his gentle presence,
we are reminded of his gracious promises, and our heavy, hurting
hearts are quieted.*

❖ ❖

God doesn't give us answers. He gives us himself.

Fredrick Beuchner

❖ ❖

Christians are not exempt from natural disasters or from the blows of those who oppose our faith. Rather, God promises grace and strength for us to endure life's inevitable agonies. No matter how we are oppressed, we can never pass beyond God's gathering embrace.

J. Edward Culpepper

168

❖ ❖

Satan attempts to defeat us by severing our spiritual supply. Yet Paul reminds us that "my God shall supply all your needs according to his riches in glory by Christ Jesus" (Philippians 4:19). So when we need strength, we have the Almighty God. When healing is needed, we have the Great Physician. When authority is required, we have the King of Kings. When peace is lacking, we have the Prince of Peace. The supply line from heaven is never blocked, and the storehouse of heaven is never depleted. Satan may try to knock us down, but his attempts to seize us will never knock us out, because we have an unlimited supply from an inexhaustible Lord.

Gene Wilder

❖ ❖

God will come in at the deepest part of the stream to lend you a hand.

Samuel Rutherford

❖ REFLECTION ❖

Think back to a time of sorrow or loss. Did you sense God's hand at the "deepest part of the stream"? How will you make yourself more open to receive God's comfort in the future?

❖ ❖

What searing difficulties are you facing right now? Do not despair. Take hope. Hope in God. Trusting in him, look honestly at your life and separate out its hopeless elements from those with possibilities. Don't let your despair over specifics contaminate what is sound and good and fruitful in your life. Hoping in God, you trust his future for you. Hoping in God, you find the strength to be patient. Hoping in God, you see him not so much a solver of problems as the maker of your life. Hoping like that takes us down paths we did not choose and calls for endurance of painful trials we seek to avoid but which lead us ever closer to him.

Colbert S. Cartwright

❖ ❖

If we really believe in God, we can dare to look the worst in the face. God is greater and stronger than anything.

James W. Cox

❧ ❧

God is good, but that does not mean that bad things won't happen. Floods come, people we love are injured, cancer strikes, marriages break up. Our hearts at times are broken. The Bible does not promise a life without tears. What God promises is that when we hurt, God cares. When we are in pain, God walks that valley with us. When we feel alone, we are not alone, because God is closer than our breath. When our heart is broken, God weeps with us. God is nearest when the pain seems unbearable.

170

❧ ❧

PROMISES

God has not promised
Skies always blue,
Flower-strewn pathways
All our lives through.
God has not promised
Sun without rain,
Joy without sorrow,
Peace without pain.
But God has promised
Strength for the day,
Rest for the laborer,

Light on the way;
Grace for the trial,
Help from above
Unfailing sympathy,
Undying love.

❖ ❖

We need your help, O Lord, not as a last resort but in every
moment we live.

❖ ❖

God cares about you, even when you feel unworthy of his care,
even when you do not care about him. God's mercy and compassion are stronger than our sin and selfishness.

J. A. Davidson

❖ ❖

God never gives up. God is always running ahead of us, trying
to catch us at unsuspecting moments, drawing us to himself.
When a person finds God, he usually experiences the strange
sensation that it is God who has actually found him.

Donald Strobe

❖ ❖

❧ PRAYER ❧

Out of our darkness we come to you for light.
Out of our sorrows we come to you for joy.
Out of our doubts we come to you for certainty.
Out of our anxieties we come to you for peace.
Out of our sin we come to you for your forgiving love.
Open your hand this day and satisfy our every need.

Disappointment

❧ ❧

The Lord is good to those who wait for him,
to the soul that seeks him. . . .
For the Lord will not reject forever.
Although he causes grief, he will have compassion
according to the abundance of his steadfast love.

LAMENTATIONS 3:25, 31-32

We do not want you to be unaware, brothers and
sisters, of the affliction we experienced in Asia; for we
were so utterly, unbearably crushed that we despaired
of life itself.

PAUL IN 2 CORINTHIANS 1:8

❧ ❧

*The Bible is filled with people who wrestled with disappointment—
disappointment with others, disappointment with themselves, and
even disappointment with God. The apostle Paul saw doors of opportunity closed in his face. The prophet Hosea watched his wife
leave him for the street life of Palestine. Jesus was betrayed by one
of his closest followers, disowned by another, and abandoned by all
of them. Job saw his family murdered and his wealth stolen. How
can we survive when those we love the most fail us, or when the God*

we trust seems to let the worst happen to us? The selections in this chapter are not easy, pious answers to our struggle with disappointment. Instead, these wise teachers help us keep our footing on the solid rock of God's unchanging love and his unfailing promises.

❖ ❖

God can do wonders with a broken heart if you give him all the pieces.

Victor Alfsen

❖ ❖

The Gospels do not portray Jesus as always the pleasant man or the peaceful man. If we think of winter as unhappiness and disappointment, then Jesus had his share and more.

David W. Richardson

❖ ❖

What do you do when you lose your job and can't find another, and all the doors of life are suddenly closed, slammed in your face, shut tight? Or when the doctor finds a lump and says that it must be removed *at once?* When someone who has been very close to you dies? What you do then reveals the kind of person you are. Do you panic? Do you fold up in a state of paralysis? Do you withdraw from the situation in fear and trembling? Do you protest and shake your fist in rage and say, "Why does this happen to me?" Or do you pray? Do you do what the psalmist did who wrote, "When I was in trouble, I called on the Lord, and he heard me?" Or do you call up someone else and ask him to call upon the Lord? These are all possibilities, but there is a more excellent way.

The first thing to do is to sit down for a half hour and do nothing at all. You can sit still and do nothing if you think something. Say to yourself these four things:

(a) Nothing can happen to me that has not happened to millions of others. I am unique; but my trouble is not unique. You shed once and for all the idea that you have been selected as a special target for life's worst blows.

(b) Then say this: I knew ahead of time that as a human being I ran the risk of something like this. One of the things that surprises me as I see people going through difficult times is that so many of them seem to be completely surprised that anything like this could happen. Adverse winds are a part of life. You are never ready for them; you are never waiting to welcome them, not if you are normal. But you can prepare yourself for the possibility that they may one day or another strike you.

(c) Then go further and say to yourself: There are people who did their greatest work when they were blown by adverse winds.

(d) The last thing you say to yourself is this: I do not know *how* I am going to handle this, but I know that I *can*. I know that, from sources of which I am not conscious, help will come—not necessarily the help I ask for, but help that I know nothing about will rise up in me, will appear suddenly from all sorts of unexpected places. If I wait quietly, that help will come. I can do all things through Christ who strengthens me.

Then you are ready to pray. That is the next thing to do. Instead of praying *for* something, pray *about* it. In one sense, you may have already been doing it. You have already been thinking about your situation in God's presence before you ask for anything. You have been draining off some of the bitterness in yourself. Then ask God for what you want. If you want a job, ask him for it. If you want help, ask him for it. If you want to win some battle, perhaps some inner battle fought behind the closed doors of your life, ask him to give you the victory. If you want to get out of a difficult situation, ask him to help get you out of it. And after you ask him, then go to work on it yourself. If you want a job, go out and look for one. You probably will not find the one you are looking for, but if you don't look, you won't find any. If you want a friend, if you feel left alone in life, be a friend to someone. You will not get what you want just for the asking. If you do nothing about it, nothing will happen. On the other hand, if you pray about it, you may get it, but you may not. You may get something even greater than what you asked for.

Theodore Parker Ferris

~ ~

God is a purposeful God. He uses even the difficult experiences of life to make us more like Jesus. No trial is ever wasted. We may not always see God's purposes, but we can always trust his care.

~ ~

God does not give up on men and women so easily or so quickly as we give up on ourselves and each other.

Wayne E. Oates

❧ ❧

Out of every disappointment there is a lesson, then a correction, a purification, and finally a reconciliation—and always beyond the ashes there is God.

Donald Stewart Miller

❧ ❧

It is a great thing for us when we have learned that even in trouble God has for us a door of hope. How many a devout servant of Christ owes the beginning of his allegiance to his Lord to a serious illness, to some crippling disappointment, or to an overwhelming sorrow. Many have been able to say with the psalmist, "It is good for me to have been afflicted." There is a door of hope even in the valley of trouble, and those who tread it in God's company will not fail to find it.

John Bishop

❧ REFLECTION ❧

Think back to a time of disappointment or trouble. In what ways can you now say, "It was good for me to have been afflicted"?

❧ ❧

The love of God remains in charge through the worst life can do to us.

James W. Crawford

❧ PRAYER ❧

I'm disappointed, Lord—disappointed in my financial situation; my mate, best friend, child, or parent; my circumstances; my church—and you seem so slow to help me! I've prayed and cried and begged, but my prayers only reach the ceiling. I know in my mind that you are near me, but I need to sense your presence and your enfolding love. If you are with me, I can survive. Amen.

Douglas Connelly

———————

"IN YOUR NAME I WILL HOPE"

HOρe

❦ ❦

Let me hear of your steadfast love in the morning,
for in you I put my trust.
Teach me the way I should go,
for to you I lift up my soul.

PSALM 143:8

We have become absolutely convinced that neither
death nor life, neither messenger of Heaven nor mon-
arch of earth, neither what happens today nor what
may happen tomorrow, neither a power from on high
nor a power from below, nor anything else in God's
whole world has any power to separate us from the love
of God in Jesus Christ our Lord!

ROMANS 8:38-39, (PHILLIPS TRANSLATION)

❖ ❖

For many people, hope is a childish wish that everything will turn
out all right in the end. It's crossing our fingers or wishing on a
star or closing our eyes to reality. But hope, in the Christian vo-
cabulary, isn't like that at all. For the Christian, hope is some-
thing certain and solid. We have confidence in the future because
we have confidence in the promises of a trustworthy God. God has

*proved himself over and over in our lives and we can rest in his
goodness and his grace.*

❧ ❧

Christians are people who hope in the midst of the most hopeless situations.

Howard L. Rice

❧ ❧

Christian hope is Resurrection hope. Powered by the engine of
Christian love and steered by the rudder of the Resurrection, it
keeps a steady course between the whirlpool of optimism and the
rocks of despair. We look forward to life in the future. We look
into our own personal future neither in optimism or despair,
knowing that whatever sorrows or trouble or doubt, whatever
grief or pain or stress, whatever loneliness or even persecution
may come, Christ is risen. Nothing in all creation can separate us
from his love.

Brian A. Wren

❧ ❧

In days of brightness, hope can be the sail that the soul spreads
to catch the favoring breeze, a sail that carries the ship over a
sunlit sea toward a sure haven. But in the dark night of storm,
hope is the anchor that plunges down through the heaving waters and holds so firmly to the rock beneath that not all the fury

of the storm can drive the vessel from its place of safety. Such is the hope that comes to us in Christ.

John Bishop

❖ ❖

The Bible pictures hope as an anchor. The storms of life can be overwhelming, but in the storm we know that God has not abandoned us and that the storm will not last forever. We are held secure by hope, by our unfailing confidence in an unfailing God.

❖ ❖

Hope is patient, recognizing that life requires us to stand up under difficult circumstances and await confidently the good that shall, in God's own time, emerge. We can trust the future because the future belongs to God. As Christians we need to see that our hope is ultimately not for anything; it not a hope that something will happen. We hope in God. To hope in specifics—counting on a good grade, getting the job, or finding the cure—is to end up at some point disappointed, bitter, angry, and unbelieving. When our specific hopes do not materialize, we conclude either that God is powerless and evil or that we have no faith. Our hope in adversity springs from trust in a loving God.

Colbert S. Cartwright

❖ ❖

Christ does not always remove or open closed doors; he may come through them.

❧ ❧

No human situation is hopeless if God is taken into account—and God is waiting for us to wait on him! He is waiting for us to realize that when we reach the end of our tether, he is there.

John H. Gladstone

❧ REFLECTION ❧

186

How would your attitude toward the future change if you were absolutely persuaded that God's plans for you were for good and not for calamity?

"For surely I know the plans I have for you, says the Lord, plans for your welfare and not for harm, to give you a future with hope" (Jeremiah 29:11).

❧ ❧

The Christian hope is not simply a trembling, hesitant hope that perhaps the promises of God may be true. It is the confident expectation that they cannot be anything else but true.

William Barclay

❧ ❧

St. Francis of Assisi is one of the most saintly people in the history of the Church. A legend has it that he came upon a beggar who was a leper. That day, following a powerful impulse, he flung himself from his horse and got down beside the beggar, taking him into his arms. As he did, the face of the beggar became the face of Christ. Here is great hope! No person walks alone; Christ walks with us. And no person suffers alone; Christ suffers with us.

Chevis F. Horne

❧ ❧

God seems to break through when circumstances appear most hope- 187
less. In the book of Revelation, John (one of Jesus' closest followers)
was exiled on the prison island of Patmos. The Christian commu-
nity was being persecuted throughout the Roman world. It looked
like the Church might be destroyed. In that hopeless situation, God
gave John a vision of things as they really were. John saw heaven
open and God was sitting on the throne of the universe. God was
not wringing his hands, wondering if everything would turn out
all right. God was ruling in triumphant victory!

❧ ❧

Men and women, things are not as they appear! We are not alone wrestling with the hosts of wickedness in high places! There is a throne in heaven, and there is one who sits upon that throne who loves us with an everlasting love, and there are those round about the throne that await his command. Thus there is at this very moment a power in the world, not our own, that makes for righteousness, and even now there is help available for each and every situation. There is a throne in heaven and God is on that throne.

S. Robert Weaver

❖ PRAYER ❖

Loving God, some of us feel as though our situation is hopeless. We ask that your Spirit would infuse our lives with hope, with the assurance of your goodness and your ultimate triumph over all that is wrong and evil. In the darkness we cling to you alone. Thank you that we are your children and that no problem is outside your attention or tender care. Amen.

Douglas Connelly

"WHY ARE YOU DOWNCAST?"

Discouragement

❧ ❧

In my distress I called upon the Lord;
to my God I cried for help.
From his temple he heard my voice,
and my cry to him reached his ears.
He reached down from on high,
he took me;
he drew me out of mighty waters.

PSALM 18:6, 16

Jesus said, "Stop having a troubled heart! You already
believe in God; now in the same way believe in me."

PARAPHRASE OF JOHN 14:1

"Come to me, all you that are weary and carrying
heavy burdens, and I will give you rest. Take my yoke
upon you, and learn from me; for I am gentle and
humble in heart, and you will find rest for your souls."

JESUS IN MATTHEW 11:28-29

❧ ❧

When I'm discouraged, I complain to the wrong people. I tell my wife how bad I feel, or I call a friend and set up a lunch appointment so I can lay the burden of my discouragement on him. These people love me, so they put up with my complaints and even try to help me, but they should not be my first line of defense against discouragement. I should go first to God.

Unfortunately, we let our reverence for God ruin a perfectly good opportunity to express how we really feel. I've heard hurting people pray and never once mention their pain! When will we learn that no one cares more about us than our Father? He knows how we feel, so he's not shocked when we tell him; and it's often in the honest telling that God brings us a sense of comfort and assurance. The way out of the dark pit of discouragement is not to put on a fake smile and pretend everything's okay. The way out is to look up and pour out our hurts to God.

192

❖ ❖

We cannot know whether our faith is equal to any test until we actually face the test! We all know people who have been able to bear the unbearable, to face and do the impossible, to rise to the heights of achievement in times of stress that seem absolutely incredible. In most instances, you will find that such people have lived with God through the days before the testing. They have developed deep reservoirs of divine strength through their own prayer and worship. They have found inspiration in, and believed the assurances of, the Bible. Faith, in a sense, is spiritual adrenaline. We keep a deposit in our lives, using a bit of it now and then

as small crises arise. Then—whammo!—comes a real crisis and
we are sent reeling across the floor. But that spiritual adrenaline
floods through our bodies and we find strength to get up and
go on. God has provided us with unexpected resources that enable us to maintain poise, to find strength, to gain courage, and
to remain confident.

Brian L. Harbour

❖ ❖

It is good for me to draw near to God;
I have put my trust in the Lord God. . . .
God is the strength of my heart
and my portion forever.

Psalm 73:23, 28

❖ ❖

What do you do when you find Jesus asleep? That's the question
of despair and desperation that comes during the crisis moments
that all of us face in life. A patient is diagnosed as having cancer.
The contract where you work is not renewed and you are laid
off, wondering how you will make ends meet. That relationship
that promised to have been made in heaven ends. It's difficult to
understand! One moment everything is going great; the next
moment the storm winds of crisis begin to blow and our world
is sinking around us. We cry out to God, "Don't you care that
we drown?" But look, he's asleep in the boat. What do you do

193

when you find Jesus asleep? The Bible says that we should rejoice that he's in the boat with us and claim the faith that he has the power to help us weather any storm!

Craig A. Loscalzo

❖ ❖

If you are discouraged, it's because you put all your trust in your own efforts and now you realize that you can't go it alone. Had you placed your trust in God, you would still feel regret for your failings, but you wouldn't be discouraged. You forget that God is as loving and as all-powerful after you've fallen as before. Discouragement is clear proof that you've placed too much confidence in yourself and too little in God.

Michael Quoist

194

❖ ❖

God has given us abundant resources for our battle against discouragement, but sometimes discouragement paralyzes us so badly that we can't pray or read the Bible or reach out to friends who will help us. It takes all our strength just to get out of bed or pack lunch for the kids. Doing the tasks at hand, however, may be the first step on the path out of the cave of despair.

❖ ❖

There is only one thing to do, then, when we are plunged into difficulty or despair. Trust and pray, and do what seems to be the immediate duty. There is great relief for depressed hearts in any kind of activity, and when one duty is done, the next will appear more clear. Help comes most unexpectedly, but not usually till we do our best and gain the mastery of our own doubts and fears.

~∗ ∗~

Weeping may lodge with us at evening, but in the morning there is a shout of joy.

Psalm 30:5, Goodspeed translation

~∗ ∗~

There are great rewards for those who will forget that which ought to be forgotten and press on; great rewards for those who are determined to take what is at hand and fashion something good from it; great rewards for those who will live their lives in service unafraid; great rewards for those who instead of remembering those who hurt them will think of those who are always waiting at the ferries of difficult streams to help them over.

M.K.W. Heicher

~∗ REFLECTION ∗~

Where do you turn first for comfort and help when you are discouraged? When do you turn to God—early in the process or when every other resource has failed?

~∗ ∗~

Why should I be discouraged,
Why should the shadows come,
Why should my heart be lonely
And long for heaven and home,
When Jesus is my portion?
My constant Friend is He;
His eye is on the sparrow,
And I know He watches me.

Civilla D. Martin

❖ PRAYER ❖

Father of lights, with whom there is no variation or shadow due to change, in the midst of this changing and confusing world, help us to put our trust in thee. By our knowledge of thee may we become steadfast and immovable, always abounding in the work of the Lord. Lift us above the breaking waves and the surging tide, above the clamor and din of the crowd, into thy peace.

M.K.W. Heicher

"A GARMENT OF PRAISE"

JOY

❧ ❧

You have turned my mourning into dancing;
you have taken off my sackcloth
and clothed me with joy,
so that my soul may praise you and not be silent.
O Lord, my God, I will give thanks to you forever.

PSALM 30:11-12

Rejoice always, pray without ceasing, give thanks
in all circumstances; for this is the will of God in
Christ Jesus for you.

1 THESSALONIANS 5:16-18

❖ ❖

*When several thousand young adults were asked, "What is your
ultimate ambition?" more than 70 percent said, "To be happy."
Unfortunately, those people will end up disappointed. Only char-
acters in fairy tales live "happily ever after." God does not promise
us happiness; he offers us joy. Happiness depends on the circumstances in which we find ourselves. A child with an earache, an
adult who has been fired in a corporate downsizing, and a spouse
who has been abandoned by a mate cannot at that time be happy.*

Joy, on the other hand, is not linked to circumstances. Christians who are in prison or who are fighting a terminal disease or who have been washed out in the latest job layoff can know a sense of joy in God's love and care. Jesus said it was like an underground spring pushing refreshing water over our lives even in our most unhappy times.

~· ·~

If there is anything that should typify Christian living, it is the quality of joy. It is never a momentary joy that comes from hearing something funny. Rather, it is a joy that comes from deep within.

James Blevins

~· ·~

The religion of the Bible is a religion of joy. You get it even long before the coming of Christ, in the book of Psalms: "Be glad in the Lord and rejoice, ye righteous, and shout for joy all ye that are upright in heart." How often the psalmists strike that note— sometimes even calling on the whole of nature to rejoice with them. And when you come to the New Testament, you will find that the word *joy* has become one of the key words of Christianity, just like *peace* and *love* and *faith*. When Paul sets out to give a list of the fruit of the Spirit, he mentions love first, as you might expect, and then he puts this more unexpected thing called joy. Paul says to his fellow Christians at Philippi, "Rejoice in the Lord always, and again I say, Rejoice." That is the Christianity of the New Testament. It is a religion of joy.

It is not that these people were living in a prosperous and tranquil age and in highly favorable circumstances, or that they went about this tragic world in blinders because they were wholly intent on the joys of the next world. Far from it! It is quite extraordinary how often we find those in the Bible saying that they were living in bad times and in an evil world. Yet underneath all that there was a deep, constant current of gladness, and that is the authentic Christianity of the New Testament.

D. M. Baillie

❖ REFLECTION ❖

Can you remember a time in your life when the circumstances in which you found yourself were unhappy but you experienced inner joy from the Lord? What insights from that time would you share with a friend who is going through a difficult time?

❖ ❖

Happiness and pleasure come and go, but the joy of God is constant. It abides through all the changing scenes and seasons of life. Happiness and pleasure have to be pursued or created, but joy cannot be fashioned by any amount of human ingenuity. It can only be received for it is a gift of the Spirit; it is a treasure graciously bestowed on us by God.

Ernle Young

❖ ❖

Happiness must come from within. It cannot come from outward circumstances. We all know people who have everything one could desire, as far as external circumstances are concerned, but who are bored, frustrated, and unhappy.

H. Richard Rasmussen

～❖ ❖～

One of the character traits of God is joy. As we become like our heavenly Father, we will exhibit more and more of his joyful, exuberant spirit.

202

～❖ ❖～

Three times in the Bible there is said to have been joy in heaven. First, there was joy in heaven when the world was created, for when the cornerstone was laid, "the morning stars sang together, and all the sons of God shouted for joy" (Job 38:7). Second, there was joy in heaven when Jesus was born in Bethlehem, for then the angel announced to the shepherds, "I am bringing you good news of great joy" (Luke 2:10). Third, there is joy in heaven when any wanderer returns, for it is Jesus who tells us that there is joy in heaven over one sinner who repents (Luke 15:7, 10).

William Barclay

～❖ ❖～

❖ REFLECTION ❖

When you think of God, do you picture him as joyful?
How would a perception of a joy-filled God change your
approach to God in prayer?

❖ ❖

Joy is the primary color of the gospel of Jesus Christ. We are not
accustomed to thinking this way, for we have stereotyped Jesus
as "a man of sorrows, and acquainted with grief." It amazes us
to think of him as a man of joy, or of the New Testament as a
joyous book. But look at the statistics: the word *joy* occurs fifty-
seven times in the New Testament, the word *sorrow* eight times,
the word *rejoice* forty-five times, the word *cross* twenty-nine
times, and the word *resurrection* forty-one times. At his first public appearance, Jesus issued a proclamation of joy: good news to
the poor, release to the captives, sight for the blind, liberty for
the oppressed. Even in the upper room, with the blackest clouds
of human history beginning to blot out the sun, he prayed that
his disciples might experience that joy that was in him. Jesus left
joy streaming behind him as he moved through life.

M.K.W. Heicher

❖ ❖

Joy in the Lord is that costly inner equilibrium, that unshakable
confidence that the Lord is always at hand and that you and I are
always in his hands, no matter what happens. It is the assurance
that he is in every event, every circumstance with us, working to

save, to heal, to forgive, to reconcile, to restore. It is the assurance that nothing is permanently lost to him or beyond the reach of his resurrection power. It is the trust that when we've done what we can do, we can give ourselves into his care, knowing that he has other hands than our own and that his work will go on when our work is finished.

Robert A. Raines

❖ PRAYER ❖

O God, we give you thanks for your care and your blessings, for the joy we experience every day in knowing you as our Father. Thank you that heaven will not be a dreary, solemn place but a feast, filled with the sounds of laughter and singing. Remind us to bring some of that heavenly joy into the lives of the people we touch, just like Jesus did. Amen.

Douglas Connelly

―――――――

"DO NOT BE AFRAID"

fear

❖ ❖

"Do not fear, for I have redeemed you;
I have called you by name,
you are mine.
When you pass through the waters,
I will be with you;
and through the rivers,
they shall not overwhelm you;
when you walk through fire
you shall not be burned,
and the flame shall not consume you.
For I am the Lord, your God."

ISAIAH 43:1B-3A

There is no fear in love, but perfect love casts out fear.

1 JOHN 4:18

"Take heart, it is I; do not be afraid."
"Get up and do not be afraid."
"Do not fear, only believe."
"Do not be afraid . . . for I am with you."
"Do not be afraid; I am the first and the last."

JESUS TO PEOPLE GRIPPED BY FEAR
(MATTHEW 14:27, 17:7; MARK 5:36; ACTS
18:9-10; REVELATION 1:17)

❧ ❧

The command repeated most often in the Bible is, "Do not fear." God has to keep reminding us that he is our provision, our power, and our protection. If all we have are our own resources to rely on, we have plenty to fear. Resting in God's care, we have nothing to fear.

❧ ❧

The best cure for shaking knees is to kneel on them.

Fredrick Donald Coggan

❧ ❧

208

Fear is a hypnotist. It says to us again and again, "You cannot, you cannot!" So fear produces what it fears. It is a creative force. Listen to it long enough and its message turns out to be true: you cannot.

Harry Emerson Fosdick

❧ ❧

The very first human emotion mentioned in the Bible is fear. When God found Adam and Eve hiding in the garden and inquired, "Why?" Adam replied, "We were afraid." Ever since then, God has been trying to get his people not to be afraid. All through the Bible, the plea is for us not to fear.

John T. Wallace

❧ ❧

Second Timothy 1:7 says, "God has not given us the spirit of fear." Fear is the opposite of faith. God has not caused us to be overcome by fear. Satan has caused that. God has given us the spirit of power, the spirit of love, and the spirit of a sound mind.

Greg Clements

❖ REFLECTION ❖

Think about the times you are most afraid. Now envision how you would feel if Jesus were in the same circumstances with you. His promise is that he will never abandon us.

❖ ❖

For the Lord to quiet the raging storms that often assault us, it is only necessary to trust him to command the winds and the rain to cease. Until calm returns, hang on in faith. Hang on to the assurance that Jesus rides with you, awake or asleep, and that you can trust him to respond to your needs. Your storm may be a nagging illness or job security or a course in school in which you fear failure. Your troublesome winds may be stirring fear due to marital problems or financial problems or death itself. Have faith, even a little, in the Christ who saves. Here is the assurance every Christian carries with him or her: Christ does not abandon ship. He knows how to ride out the storm; but more than that, he knows how to quiet its surge and defuse its power, taming its waves by silencing its winds.

Richard Andersen

❖ ❖

When the storm arose, Jesus was in the boat with the disciples. He wasn't off at a distance as a casual observer; he was right in the middle of their crisis, as he is always a part of our crises, even though at times he appears to be sleeping. What do you do when you find Jesus asleep? We should rejoice that he is in the boat with us and claim the faith that he has the power to help us weather any storm!

Craig A. Loscalzo

❖ ❖

God watches as we pass through the experiences of life. He examines our response to each new challenge. Will we respond with faith or with fear?

❖ ❖

I sought the Lord and he heard me, and delivered me from all my fears.

Psalm 34:4

❖ ❖

Over the fireplace of an old inn in England there is a motto: "Fear knocked at the door. Faith answered. There was no one there."

❖ ❖

Fear is banished by Jesus' healing touch. Like an illness, fear requires healing. Jesus was and is the Great Physician. Fear meets its match in him. What happens is that divine strength is imparted, taking over where our strength ends.

John H. Townsend

❧ ❧

In her autobiography, Corrie ten Boom tells of the experiences of her Dutch family during the Nazi occupation. Defiantly they hid Jews in their home and helped them to escape certain death. The ten Booms knew they were risking capture and probably death, so one day young Corrie blurted to her father, "I need you. You can't die, you can't." Her father responded, "Corrie, when you and I go to Amsterdam, when do I give you your ticket?" The child replied, "Why, just before we get on the train." "Exactly, and our wise Father in heaven knows when we are going to need things, too. Don't run ahead of him, Corrie. When the time comes that some of us will have to die, you will look into your heart and find the strength you need, just in time."

❧ PRAYER ❧

Today, heavenly Father, banish our fears. Give us faith strong enough to face whatever darkness may confront us, and to face it with courage, knowing that both darkness and light are the same with you, and that no creature of the shadows is greater than you.

"NEITHER DO I CONDEMN YOU"

failure
and guilt

❖ ❖

The Lord is good,
a stronghold in a day of trouble;
he protects those who take refuge in him.

NAHUM 1:7

God is greater than our hearts.

1 JOHN 3:20

❧ ❧

Failure is one of life's uglies, along with its sidekick, guilt. These two enemies can frighten us, paralyze us, and even destroy us. The good news is that we don't have to live under their control any longer! The Spirit-filled response to failure is not just to look on the bright side. The answer to failure is to see that God stands on the other side of the failure, ready to take our worst losses and turn them into gains.

❧ ❧

God uses broken things. It takes broken soil to produce a crop, broken clouds to give rain, broken grain to give bread, broken bread to give strength. It is the broken alabaster box in the Gospels that gives out its perfume. It is Peter, weeping bitterly, who returns to greater power than ever.

Vance Havner

❖ ❖

Atonement for us means that God, through Christ, saw beyond our sin, beyond our ugliness, our unlovableness, our rebellion, and died that we might be redeemed, restored, reconciled. Sin had discarded us; it had put the scars of its following on us; the flaws from disobedience were evident. But redemption is God coming to us, in his Son, and touching all the scars and flaws with atoning healing, lifting life to possibility and hope.

214

C. Neil Strait

❖ ❖

Jesus had a way of looking deep into the hearts of those he met. He never judged a person for what he was or what he had been. He always looked at a person and saw him for what he might become.

Hoover Rupert

❖ ❖

THE LAND OF BEGINNING AGAIN

I wish there were some wonderful place,
Called the Land of Beginning Again,
Where all our mistakes and all our heartaches
And all our selfish grief,
Could be dropped like a shabby coat at the door,
And never put on again.

Louisa Fletcher Tarkington

❧ ☙

With God, failure is never final.

John Short

❧ ☙

Sometimes it is not the failure that terrorizes us but the guilt we feel because of our failure. We can't seem to get beyond the shame and stupidity of our sin.

❧ ☙

Nothing can so keep us near to the fountain of God's forgiving grace as the memory of sin. It can keep us on our knees in a great dependence on him.

James Reid

❧ ☙

The experience of guilt is a sign that God is not through with us. Guilt is a token of God's continuing respect for our possibilities. It tells us why the siren of conscience is ringing so loudly within us. Guilt is also a call from God to help us repent and seek forgiveness. It is God's way to remind us that we were made for something better than sin. God made it possible for us to rise from our failures.

James Earl Massey

❖ ❖

Accept the fact that you've made some failures, but you are not a failure. You are in the process of becoming. You need not accept yourself as a failure. You become a failure only when you do not use your failures as stepping stones to success.

M.K.W. Heicher

❖ REFLECTION ❖

Think about some failure or regret that you look back on with shame. If you could release that failure to God's forgiving grace, how would you feel? How would it allow you to live your life differently?

❖ ❖

God risks our failures and our sins. He allows folly and failure to exist so that genuine faith may develop in the laboratory of life. They both flourish in the same soil. Those who are perennially disappointed in God's response to their plights view God as a giant Mr. Fix-it. They want this overindulgent parent to walk into their playrooms and repair the toys they and their friends have carelessly demolished. But God is more like a waiting father who allows his prodigal children to drift into the far country in hopes that they will grow up there and eventually return to him. I don't know about you, but I would rather be a prodigal who has the possibilities of becoming a real son than a puppet on a string!

James E. Sorrell

❧ ❧

God's response to our failure is not shock or surprise; he responds 217
with mercy and grace—and another chance. God can take the most
tragic situation, like the execution of his own Son, and bring glory
and good out of it.

❧ ❧

There is something gripping about a God who can spring a surprise like the cross; if he could turn that to good, we may believe that even the worst features of our lives may be used by him for good also.

M.K.W. Heicher

❧ ❧

Christ is in the business of redeeming our mistakes. He transforms them. He overcomes them. He adds later chapters to them that allow us to go on and leave them behind. He brings us to life beyond our mistakes.

Bob Woods

❧ ❧

The past cannot be changed; the future is still in your power.

❧ ❧

Don't dwell on what you can't do anything about. Paul calls this "forgetting what lies behind." The hesitation, distraction, and wasted effort involved in gazing backward hinder advancement. That is especially true when you are concentrating on past failures.

Donald A. Spieler

❧ ❧

Where we write "The end," God writes, "To be continued."

Herbert Gezork

❧ ❧

❖ PRAYER ❖

Understanding Father, God of gentle forgiveness, hear
now our confession of sin and desire for recovery and
cleansing. We call you light, but walk too often in darkness; we call you peace, but do violence to others, to your
creation, and even to ourselves; we call you joy, yet live
our days in sadness and even bitterness; we call you hope,
but spend our days stumbling in despair; we call you love,
yet despise others, crouch in fear, and harbor distrust in
our hearts. Lord Jesus, who has borne our pain and car-
ried our sorrows away, who has suffered and died for our
sins, forgive us again and restore us to rightness and one-
ness with you, with others, and with ourselves.

William M. Johnson

"LOVE NEVER FAILS"

Love for others

❧ ❧

As God's chosen ones, holy and beloved, clothe yourselves with compassion, kindness, humility, meekness,
and patience. Above all, clothe yourselves with love,
which binds everything together in perfect harmony.

COLOSSIANS 3:12, 14

Do not rejoice when your enemies fall,
and do not let your heart be glad when they stumble.

PROVERBS 24:17

We love because he first loved us.

1 JOHN 4:19

❖ ❖

*Some people think of love only in terms of warm, bubbly feelings or
waves of romantic longing. The love God calls us to display, however, is tougher than an emotional impulse. Genuine love loves the
unloving and unlovely; it's a love that chooses to act for the good
of the other person, regardless of that person's response.*

*We don't find it hard to love those who love us. The rub comes
when we are expected to love our neighbor or our enemy. How hard*

is it to love your spouse when he or she isn't very loveable, or to love other Christians when they have wounded you? But that is precisely what God empowers us to do. God can expect that level of love from us because he loved us with an infinite love even when we were disobedient and far from him.

❧ ❧

To love at all is to be vulnerable. Love anything, and your heart will certainly be wrung and possibly broken. If you want to make sure of keeping it intact, you must give your heart to no one, not even to an animal. Wrap it carefully with hobbies and little luxuries, avoid all entanglements, lock it up safe in the casket of your selfishness. But in that casket—safe, dark, motionless, airless—it will change. It will not be broken; it will become unbreakable, impenetrable, irredeemable. The only place outside heaven where you can be perfectly safe from all the dangers of love is hell.

C. S. Lewis

❧ ❧

Love can never sit by contentedly and see the one it loves perish. It has no choice but to forget itself and seek to do something to remedy the situation. At the risk of its own destruction, it rushes into the burning building to rescue the trapped child. At the endangering of its own life, it nurses tenderly the loved one who has become the victim of a contagious and deadly dis-

222

ease. Love always acts to prevent its beloved from perishing. It dies in the attempt sometimes, but it acts.

Roy H. Short

❧ ❧

The way to get rid of your enemies is not to destroy them but to make them your friends. Genuine love is imaginative. It returns good for evil. It prays for those who slight you or irritate you. It turns the other cheek. It goes a second mile.

John Thompson

❧ REFLECTION ❧

Think of someone to whom you can demonstrate genuine love in the next twenty-four hours. Move beyond family or close friends to someone at the edge of your circle of acquaintances. God may even bring an enemy to mind. Reflect on how you can act for that person's benefit. It may be a small step—speaking a kind word or writing a note of appreciation or simply praying for the person. One small step of love makes the next step easier.

❧ ❧

The truth of the matter is that un-self-seeking love is our response to the love of Christ. "We love him," as John said, "because he first loved us," and in response we love those who are precious to him. We are vulnerable to the needs of others because he was first vulnerable to our need. Stand yourself in the presence of the cross when you are tempted to be inconsiderate or even brutal, and you will respond to the unlovely with grace and to the disagreeable with goodwill. You will do it not in your own name but in the name of Christ.

Harold Blake Walker

❧ ☙

Love never calculates how little it can get by with. True love's one desire is to give to the uttermost limits, and when it thinks it has given all there is to be given, wants to give even more.

Ron E. Blankenship

224

❧ ☙

Jesus wanted his followers to be marked by a unique quality: they were to love each other. Love takes a group of people from all social and economic levels, from various racial and ethnic backgrounds, and from different political persuasions, and binds that group together as one body.

❧ ☙

Love is what we do to people who irritate us.

Ray Stedman

❧ ☙

You don't have to be beautiful or handsome to love. You have to be committed. Which gospel do you hear? The gospel of the mass media? "A new commandment I give unto you that you make yourself very attractive and you shall receive love." Or the gospel of Jesus Christ? "A new commandment I give unto you that you love one another, even as I have loved you."

Bruce H. Brooke

❧ ❧

There are risks involved in loving. When those you love suffer, you will suffer with them. And when those you love reject your love, you will suffer. But if you do not give your love to others, you cannot be the complete person God intends you to be, and your life will be empty. Risk loving and be fulfilled.

225

Elmer A. Thompson

❧ ❧

Christians grow and thrive only in the company of other Christians—groves of them, known as churches. We get reinforcement, strength, and encouragement from others.

Gary C. Redding

❧ ❧

The test of our commitment to love others comes when we are wounded or ignored or abandoned. The mark of a follower of Jesus is that we put our own pain aside in order to reconcile with those who have hurt us most deeply.

❧ ❧

Jesus said, Spare no effort in making things right with your brother.

Arthur L. Walker Jr.

❖ ❖

If, then, you bear a hatred toward anyone, overcome it by doing that person a favor.

Fulton J. Sheen

❖ ❖

226 Trouble, of course, teaches us two lessons about people. The bitter lesson is that some of the people you think are your friends can let you down. That discovery can be the heaviest blow imaginable. But it is far outweighed by another discovery: that quite ordinary men and women are capable of love and loyalty and self-sacrifice for which they ask nothing in return except the knowledge that they have been of help to someone who needed them.

❖ ❖

Here is the acid test of genuine love: its ability to forgive.

Charles P. Robson

❖ ❖

The apostle Paul composed a beautiful hymn in praise of genuine love and recorded it in 1 Corinthians 13: "Love is patient; love is kind; love is not envious or boastful or arrogant or rude. It does not insist on its own way; it is not irritable or resentful; it does not rejoice in wrongdoing, but rejoices in the truth. It bears all things, believes all things, hopes all things, endures all things. Love never ends" (vv. 4–8).

❖ REFLECTION ❖

Read the passage from 1 Corinthians 13 again but substitute the name *Jesus* for the word *love* and the word *it*. That's how Jesus is toward us!

Read it a third time and put your own name in place of the word *love*. How accurately does that reflect your character and actions?

227

❖ ❖

Love is a gift, take it, let it grow.
Love is a sign we should wear, let it show.
Love is an act, do it, let it go.

William Penn

❖ PRAYER ❖

Lord, we confess that we aren't very much like Jesus. We love those who love us back, but when it comes to the unlovable, we turn away. Renew in us a commitment to love those around us as you have loved us. Give us a willingness to choose to act for their good, even when we don't feel like it. Amen.

Douglas Connelly

―――――――

"DO NOT BE
ANXIOUS ABOUT ANYTHING"

Worry

❧ ❧

Wait for the Lord;
be strong, and let your heart take courage;
wait for the Lord!

PSALM 27:14

Humble yourselves therefore under the mighty hand
of God, so that he may exalt you in due time. Cast all
your anxiety on him, because he cares for you.

1 PETER 5:6-7

"Therefore I tell you, do not worry about your life,
what you will eat, or about your body, what you will
wear. For life is more than food, and the body more
than clothing."

JESUS IN LUKE 12:22

❖ ❖

*My aunt used to say, "I'm so worried I can't think straight"—
and she was right! The word for worry and anxiety used in the
Bible means "to be divided or distracted." It describes people who*

are so upset about life's circumstances that their minds are pulled away from what they should be doing.

On several occasions, Jesus reminded his followers that worry never resolves anything. It's a completely useless activity. In fact, overblown worry is a mark of the person who doesn't trust God. "If the Father cares for the lilies and the birds," Jesus said, "why have you convinced yourself that he won't take care of you?" Worry makes us forget our incredible value to God. It makes us feel worthless and unimportant. Worry distracts our minds from God's provision and protection.

❧ ❧

230
—

If we began to think of all that could go wrong tomorrow, we would hardly dare to get up in the morning. We could be involved in an accident and lose all we hope to gain. Begin to think for five minutes about the bad things that might take place, and every bit of courage will drain away, leaving only despair and anxiety. How can we find a cure for our fear of tomorrow? The Bible finds it by contemplating the greatness of God. The Bible is telling us that there is someone in charge of this universe and of our lives. Things may seem out of hand to us, but in the end there is a person who rules the world and holds it in his hands.

Gerald Kennedy

❧ ❧

Worry is really practical atheism. It is distrust of God. If you trust, you do not worry. If you worry, you do not trust.

John H. Gladstone

❧ ❧

I have a problem with what I call the sentimental approach to worry. This approach says just keep on smiling and everything will be all right. You will need more than positive thinking when the world comes crashing in around your ears. You'll need God.

Alton H. McEachern

❧ ❧

231

Those of us who worry are daily declaring to all around that however good God has been to us in the past, we will no longer trust him in the future. This is an entire lack of faith; to our sin of faithlessness we are adding a further sin of ingratitude to God for his countless mercies of past years.

G. Lacey May

❧ REFLECTION ❧

Worry has a way of erasing God's promises from our minds. To help focus your thoughts on God's care and provision, write some of God's promises in a journal or on a card you carry with you. When worry attacks, look

at what you've written and remind yourself of God's enfolding love. Here are a couple biblical promises you can
start with:

> "Do not fear, for I am with you,
> do not be afraid, for I am your God;
> I will strengthen you, I will help you,
> I will uphold you with my victorious
>   right hand."

Isaiah 41:10

> Cast your burden on the Lord,
> and he will sustain you.

Psalm 55:22

If you have trouble sleeping, meditate on Psalm 4:8:

> I will both lie down and sleep in peace;
> for you alone, O Lord, make me lie
>   down in safety.

❧ ❧

I would suggest that we forget our worries. That is not to say
we should never have any concern about tomorrow. Intelligent
concern and plans are necessary. But a lot of people have needless worry that nags at them, cripples them, and crushes them

down to the ground. Constant worry is an affirmation that we really do not believe in the care and presence of God.

William Powell Tuck

❧ ❧

Those of us who are prone to worry waste a lot of our time thinking about the two days we can't change: yesterday and tomorrow. We can't change yesterday. If we've failed, we seek forgiveness and move on. We can't change tomorrow until it gets here. Accept the reality that every day has its own supply of problems. There's no point in taking tomorrow's problems on credit today—and that's exactly what we do when we worry.

233

❧ ❧

Don't be afraid of the day you have never seen.

❧ ❧

Tomorrow? What do you know about tomorrow? The only time that belongs to you is today. This is the acceptable time.

❧ ❧

Leave tomorrow's troubles to tomorrow's strength, tomorrow's work to tomorrow's time, tomorrow's sorrows to tomorrow's grace, and all of it to tomorrow's God.

Jack Key

❧ ❧

What does your anxiety do? It does not empty tomorrow of its sorrow, but it empties today of its strength. It does not make you escape the coming evil, but it makes you unfit to cope with it when it comes. It does not bless tomorrow, and it robs today. For every day has its own burden. God gives us power to bear all the sorrow of his making, but he does not give us the power to bear the sorrows of our own making, which the anticipation of sorrow most assuredly is.

Ian Maclaren

❧ ❧

234 We do so much fretting and regretting about things that cannot be changed, we do not have the will or energy left to change the things that can be.

John Thompson

❧ PRAYER ❧

Father, the concern on my heart today seems overwhelming. When I'm in the car, my mind is focused on my worry. When I lie awake at night, my worry is written on the ceiling. When I pray, I find myself pulled away by the concern that presses so heavily on my heart. Help me, Lord, to lay my concerns next to your unfailing promises, and as often as I think of one, remind me of the other. Amen.

Douglas Connelly

"AN EVER-PRESENT HELP"

peace

❖ ❖

Let the peace of Christ rule in your hearts.

COLOSSIANS 3:15

God will speak peace to his people,
to his faithful, to those who turn to him in their hearts.

PSALM 85:8

May the Lord bless his people with peace!

PSALM 29:11

❖ ❖

*We think of peace as the absence of something. Political peace is
the absence of war. Marital peace is the absence of conflict. A ha-
rassed parent trying to deal with three rowdy children just wants
a little "peace and quiet"—the absence of noise and turmoil.*

*The peace promised in the Bible focuses on the presence of some-
thing, or someone—the presence of God. The best word to express that
full and positive peace is the Hebrew word shalom. It means wholeness, integrity, harmony—a person in a right relationship with God
and with other human beings. External circumstances may be full*

of conflict and difficulty, but if we are centered on God, we will ex-
perience an inner calm.

❧ ☙

The peace we need is an inside job.

Denise Turner

❧ ☙

If God reigns, then his Kingdom is here and now. This, of course, seems like a paradox, for the world is anything but Christian. Yet in truth the Kingdom is both here and now, and it is also coming. For while the Kingdom of God on earth has yet to be realized, the Kingdom of God is within you. And that means, surely, that we can enjoy all the benefits of that Kingdom now. Even in a world torn with strife, we can enjoy peace.

❧ ☙

Life and death, angels and principalities and powers, things present and things to come, height and depth and every other creature—all these are declared in the Bible to be powerless to separate us from the love of God in Christ. No nook or crevice is left in the universe in which an enemy can hide. Things present—all that is now going on around us, however it may try our faith—are in the hands of God for our good. And things to come—the untrodden way before us, the hidden possibilities of the future—how these fill us with doubt and distress! But the whole boundless future contains nothing that can change God's love for us or snatch us out of his hand. It is absolutely secure, and we may rest in perfect peace.

❧ ❧

Those who try to build up security by increasing their possessions often find that they have only increased the burden of their anxieties.

❧ REFLECTION ❧

In what area of your life do you most need peace right now? Envision how you could change that troubling situation or relationship if you invited Christ into it. How can you claim his presence by faith today?

239

❧ ❧

Our days come to us not all at once but singly. We do not have to meet them all at once. But one by one, as they come to us, by God's grace we can meet them and overcome the difficulties.

❧ ❧

In the thirty-seventh Psalm, there is a man who has a wonderful secret to share with us. Here is a man very much like ourselves, all concerned about world conditions and the evil he sees around him. And then, when he is at the breaking point, God takes him by the hand and speaks to him. "Don't be so fretful about evil. Instead, trust in the Lord, delight in the Lord, commit your way to the Lord. Above all, rest in the Lord and wait patiently for him." If only we could learn to do that!

Aaron Meckel

❧ ❧

The fruit of silence is prayer;
the fruit of prayer is faith;
the fruit of faith is love;
the fruit of love is service;
the fruit of service is peace.

240

Mother Teresa

❧ ❧

I have read in Plato and Cicero many sayings that are very wise and very beautiful, but I never read in either of them such words as these: "Come unto me, all ye that labor and are heavy laden, and I will give you rest."

Saint Augustine

❧ ❧

Peace is a gift. Jesus promised his peace when the circumstances in his own life were most threatening. Just before he faced the cross, Jesus said to his followers, "My peace I give you, not as the world gives do I give to you" (John 14:27). Our jobs or bank accounts or personal interests cannot give that kind of peace. Jesus said that we are foolish to seek genuine peace in the world around us. True wholeness comes from Jesus, who offers it as the alternative to fear and distress. That's why Jesus follows his promise of peace with this command: "Stop having a troubled heart and stop being afraid!"

❧ ❧

Rest on the pillow of God's love, or to put it in an old-fashioned way, rest on the promises of God. Take your Bible; turn over its pages; seek for the promises of God. You will find them. You might find this one: "Be strong and of good courage; be not afraid, neither be dismayed; for the Lord your God is with you wherever you go." When you lay your head on that pillow to-night, you will not be afraid of anything that you may meet tomorrow. Refresh your soul on the pillow of Christ's grace. Sin is a bad pillow, but forgiveness is a good one. Worry is a restless pillow. "My peace I give to you," said Jesus. Sweet sleep comes to those who rest on that pillow.

M.K.W. Heicher

❧ PRAYER ❧

Father, we seem to rush into your presence, breathless with our wants and needs, only to rush out again just as stressed and frustrated as we were before. Calm our spirits. Allow us to rest for a few moments in your presence. Help us not just to talk but to wait—and to listen. Then perhaps we will see more clearly what our needs really are. Amen.

Douglas Connelly

THE AUTHOR

DOUGLAS CONNELLY has been a pastor and teacher for more than twenty-five years. He is the author of several best-selling books and Bible study guides, including *Angels Around Us* and *The Bible for Blockheads*. Doug lives with his wife, Karen, in Flushing, Michigan.